Promoting Effective Homicide Investigations

August 2007

This project was supported by Cooperative Agreement Number 2005-CK-WX-K011 awarded by the Office of Community Oriented Policing services, U.S. Department of Justice. The opinions contained herein do not necessarily represent the official position or policies of the U.S. Department of Justice or the members of Police Executive Research Forum. Rather, the references are illustrations to supplement discussion of the issues.

The opinions expressed are generally those based on the consensus of executive session attendees; however, not every view or statement presented in this report can necessarily be attributed to each participant.

Web sites and sources listed provide useful information at the time of this writing, but the authors do not endorse any information of the sponsor organization or other information on the web sites. The Internet references cited in this publication were valid as of August 2007. Given that URLs and web sites are in constant flux, neither the author(s) nor the COPS Office can vouch for their current validity.

U.S. Department of Justice Office of Community Oriented Policing Services

August 2007

Contents

Foreword i
Acknowledgments iii

CHAPTER 1
Introduction 1

CHAPTER 2
Homicides and Clearance Rates 7

CHAPTER 3
Managing Homicide Units for Effectiveness 19

CHAPTER 4
Eyewitness Identification 35

CHAPTER 5
Videotaped Interrogations 61

CHAPTER 6
DNA, Crime Labs, and Law Enforcement 81

CHAPTER 7
Cold Case Investigations 101

About the Authors 117
About the COPS Office 121
About PERF 123

APPENDIX A
Conference Participants 125

APPENDIX B
External Resources and Strategies for Homicide Units 135

APPENDIX C
Guidelines for Preparing and Conducting
Photo and Live Lineup Identification Procedures 137

APPENDIX D
Charlotte-Mecklenburg Police Department
Eyewitness Identification Procedures 149

APPENDIX E
Denver Police Department
Standard Operating Procedure and
Training Bulletin for Videotaping Interrogations 159

APPENDIX F
Las Vegas Metropolitan Police Department
Cold Case Solvability Criteria 171

APPENDIX G
Washington, D.C., Metropolitan Police Department
Homicide Case Review Solvability Chart 173

Foreword

MANY PROJECT IDEAS BEGIN WITH INFORMAL DISCUSSIONS among Police Executive Research Forum (PERF) members. Such instances serve to remind us how much we value the relationships we share with our members and the importance of their input. In this case, discussions with chiefs and sheriffs across the nation alerted us to two alarming trends: it seemed that in many places violent crimes were on the rise, while at the same time, homicide clearance rates were decreasing. With the support of the Office of Community Oriented Policing Services (the COPS Office), PERF hosted *Promoting Effective Homicide Investigations,* a 2-day conference in May 2006. The conference had two goals: to bring together practitioners and academics to discuss possible causes behind the decrease in clearance rates, and to present promising practices that individual law enforcement agencies have used to address the issue.

Dr. Albert P. Cardarelli (University of Massachusetts, Boston) and Dr. Charles Wellford (University of Maryland, College Park) opened the conference by presenting their research to help illuminate the consequences of unsolved murders and the variables that have contributed to the decline in clearance rates. Their research revealed that the changing nature of crime, the decentralization of police departments, and the rise in gang violence have all had an impact on the effectiveness of homicide investigations.

Law enforcement executives, academics, attorneys, and federal government representatives addressed the different effective strategies that have been developed to combat these problems, including various management and personnel decisions, videotaping suspect interviews, considering the availability of eyewitness identification options (simultaneous lineups versus sequential lineups), DNA analysis, and using cold case units and crime analysts to increase clearance rates. Case studies presented at the conference highlighted both the strengths and weaknesses associated with various investigation techniques. A town hall forum allowed attendees to discuss variables that contribute to an effective homicide unit. A lively discussion ensued, with participants mainly focusing on the role of science and technology, specifically how technology may at first appear to complicate the process but ultimately assists law enforcement by fostering change and improving investigational methods.

PERF and the COPS Office hope that this publication will help law enforcement officials determine which promising practices are the most appropriate for their departments. It has been our pleasure to facilitate and summarize the discussion for the benefit of all.

Chuck Wexler
Executive Director
Police Executive Research Forum

Carl R. Peed
Director
The COPS Office

Acknowledgments

WE THANK THE MANY PEOPLE WHO HAVE CONTRIBUTED TO this project and publication. It has been a collaborative effort, made possible by the collective experiences and insight offered by all those involved. We thoroughly enjoyed working with police executives, homicide detectives, and others committed to improving safety within our communities through the prevention and solving of violent crime. It is our hope that this book will help police leaders and investigators make informed decisions as they develop and implement initiatives aimed at improving homicide investigations. Further, we hope this publication will help to decrease crime.

Thanks are due to our sponsors at the Office of Community Oriented Policing Services for their support of the Promoting Effective Homicide Investigations Project. The COPS Office has been a steadfast supporter of PERF for many years. We are grateful to COPS Director Carl Peed, former Deputy Director Pam Cammarata, and Amy Schapiro, Senior Social Scientist Analyst and Program Manager, for their support of this project, their encouragement, and their patience. Once again the COPS Office has risen to the occasion to put resources where law enforcement needs them.

We also thank law enforcement professionals and other distinguished guests who worked closely with us on current homicide investigative initiatives as well as those who gathered in Washington, D.C., for the conference to offer comments and bring a sharp focus to the issues at hand (see Appendix A for list of attendees). A special thanks to the presenters Patricia Bailey, Assistant District Attorney, New York; Dr. Albert P. Cardarelli, Senior Fellow (Emeritus), University of Massachusetts, Boston; Jung-Won Choi, Assistant General Counsel, FBI; Deputy Superintendent Daniel Coleman, Boston Police Department; James Doyle, Director, Center for Modern Forensic Practice, John Jay College of Criminal Justice; Assistant Director Larry Ford, ATF; J.R. Francomano,

Assistant State's Attorney, Baltimore County State Attorney's Office; Special Agent Brad Garrett, FBI; Captain Tag Gleason, Seattle Police Department; Sheila Hargis, Crime Analysis Supervisor, Austin, Texas Police Department; Alan Harris, Attorney, Hennepin County, Minnesota Attorney's Office; Chief Nannette Hegerty, Milwaukee Police Department; Irvin Litofsky, Director, Forensic Services Section, Baltimore County Police Department; Maria Maher, Chief, Detectives Division, Chicago Police Department; Assistant Chief Walter Martin, Detroit Police Department; Sheri Mecklenburg, General Counsel to Superintendent, Chicago Police Department; Dr. Mallory O'Brien, Project Director, Milwaukee Homicide Review Commission, Harvard Injury Control Research Center; Deputy Chief Brian O'Keefe, Milwaukee Police Department; Lieutenant Jonathyn Priest, Denver Police Department; Dr. Nancy Steblay, Augsburg College; Detective Jim Trainum, Washington, D.C., Metropolitan Police Department; Assistant Chief Louis Vega, Miami Police Department; Dr. Charles Wellford, University of Maryland; and Captain Paul J. Zinkann III, Charlotte-Mecklenburg, North Carolina, Police Department.

In addition, we thank the contributors to each chapter in this publication. This publication would not have been possible without their valuable contributions. Also playing a critical role were many individuals who were interviewed or who reviewed various sections of the book, providing insights and suggestions. Chuck Ramsey, former chief of the Washington Metropolitan Police Department, reviewed the entire draft and made important contributions.

Of course, this book could not have been produced without the efforts of our talented and dedicated PERF staff and support personnel. Executive Director Chuck Wexler guided this project from start to finish, providing insights and resources and moderating our conference. Craig Fischer served as our senior editor. He patiently reviewed drafts, and his keen eye made this a better publication. Corina Solé Brito organized and edited early drafts of the document. Jason Cheney and Rebecca Neuburger coordinated the conference. Emily Milstein-Greengart and Alison Pastor performed information searches and provided organizational assistance.

This project traversed so many topics, departments and experts that we may have inadvertently left a contributor out. If so, we sincerely apologize.

Lisa L. Spahr
Police Executive
Research Forum

Gerard R. Murphy
Police Executive
Research Forum

1

Introduction

CALL FOR ACTION

In 2006, the Police Executive Research Forum (PERF) hosted two conferences addressing violent crime: the "Promoting Effective Homicide Investigations" (May 25 and 26) and the "National Violent Crime Summit" (August 30). Both were instrumental in understanding violent crime in the United States, as well as national and local initiatives to reduce it.[1] The primary goal of this document is to improve homicide investigations by exploring law enforcement agency practices and examining relatively new procedures that may lead to more effective investigations.

The Federal Bureau of Investigation's (FBI) report of 2005 crime data showed a 2.4 percent nationwide increase in homicides from 2004. The FBI's preliminary numbers for 2006 indicate a continued upward trend in homicides in cities across the nation. For example, during the period 2004 to 2006, homicides increased by 38 percent in Cleveland. Other cities with significant increases in homicides in that period include Cincinnati (41 percent), Houston (37 percent), Las Vegas (16 percent), Memphis (39 percent), Newark, New Jersey (25 percent), Orlando (188 percent), Philadelphia (22 percent), and Seattle (25 percent).

In light of these increases, police agencies not only need to increase their efforts to prevent homicides and focus the public's attention on the

---

1. *A Gathering Storm—Violent Crime in America*. Washington, D.C.: Police Executive Research Forum, October 2006.

violent crime problem; they also need to adopt best practices that can increase the effectiveness of homicide investigations.

THE CHANGING NATURE OF HOMICIDE INVESTIGATIONS

Homicide clearance rates in police departments are decreasing. In 1965, the average national clearance rate for homicide was 91 percent; in 1976 it was 79 percent; and in 2002 it was 64 percent. Many practitioners attribute the declining clearance rates to several factors: an increase in stranger-to-stranger homicides, which are usually more difficult to solve than cases in which the perpetrator knows the victim; gang-related offenses that turn fatal; community and witness intimidation; and reductions in witness cooperation.

Police departments also report that increasing numbers of "petty arguments" and incidents of "disrespect" lead to homicides. And other homicides are motivated by "eye for an eye" retribution. More robberies are ending in homicide, even when victims are compliant, handing over money and other valuables. The face of violence also has evolved as young people, including more females, resort to greater levels of violence. Another factor is the reentry of prisoners into communities, which increases the number of persons prone to violence.

It is important to note that the decline in clearance rates may also be the result of organizational changes in law enforcement agencies. These may include changes in the structure and placement of homicide units within the agency (e.g., decentralization in some localities), lack of resources, substantial turnover of experienced personnel, poor working relationships with prosecutors and crime labs, inability to keep pace with advances in forensic technology, and poor procedures for processing and analyzing evidence. Additionally, backlogs and heavy caseloads within crime labs and coroners' offices may reduce investigative effectiveness. The length of time it takes to get results of DNA analysis leaves offenders on the street to perhaps kill again or become victims themselves through retaliation. The combination of increased numbers of homi-

---

2. There was a slight increase in homicide clearance rates from 1993 (62 percent) to 1999 (69 percent), as the stranger-to-stranger homicide rate dropped rather sharply over this period. These numbers are drawn from the Uniform Crime Reports (UCR) for these years.

cides and decreased clearance rates also has an effect on law enforcement personnel, including physical and emotional strain and decreased morale.

Unsolved homicides have devastating effects on the family members and friends of the victims. These cases can also increase fear and anxiety in the community. The proliferation of gang-related homicides in many urban areas has made witnesses and residents reluctant to cooperate with law enforcement out of fear of retaliation. This fear, left unchecked, can hinder the ability of law enforcement to gather evidence and information in other homicides.

STRENGTHENING THE INVESTIGATIVE FUNCTION

The criminal investigative function—the process by which officers collect evidence, interview people, and compile facts for the purpose of supporting a prosecution—has always been viewed as the most challenging of all police work. Today this function seems more complex than ever. Technological developments, behavioral science research, closer scrutiny of law enforcement practices by outside parties, staffing shortages, insufficient forensic analysis resources, and a lack of universal performance indicators are some of the issues that confront law enforcement administrators and investigators.

Just since the beginning of 2005, many agencies have grappled with investigative challenges. For example, in Washington, D.C., then-Police Chief Charles H. Ramsey, then-Mayor Anthony Williams, and the City Council engaged in a very public debate over whether criminal investigators should be videotaping suspect interrogations. Harold Hurtt, shortly after being named Houston police chief, called for a moratorium on Harris County capital punishment in cases where DNA evidence was instrumental in a conviction because of problems with the police department's crime lab (see Chapter 6 for a more detailed discussion). In Boston, then-Commissioner Kathleen O'Toole overhauled procedures for witness identification of suspects, relying on recommendations from the U.S. Department of Justice for the blind administration of photo arrays.

Technological advances can be viewed as a double-edged sword by law enforcement because they are capable of helping to convict a suspect but also have the potential to expose law enforcement shortcomings or errors. Many law enforcement departments now videotape interrogations, but a large number still do not. Those that do videotape face a series of difficult questions, including when and how to videotape and what equipment to use.

Scientific advances in DNA research have contributed to the accurate identification of offenders, but the required scientific protocols have raised similar questions for departments about when and how to collect, analyze, and store DNA samples.

Psychological research has documented the subjective nature of human interaction—including how people hold biases—especially regarding crime and disorder. These biases can affect law enforcement work, too, and have affected the long-held procedures by which officers conduct lineups and arrange photo arrays for witness and victims.

These are just some examples of how the investigative process has grown more complex. American law enforcement agencies are struggling to find answers to the questions posed above as they strive to conduct rigorous and objective investigations that contribute to accurate convictions. Videotaping interrogations, using sequential photo lineups, and knowing how to use DNA effectively can help investigators identify suspects, prosecute the guilty, and exonerate the innocent.

Some agencies have adopted innovative investigative policies and practices to improve their clearance rates. These agencies realize that an effective homicide unit is more than the sum of particular resources and talented investigators. An effective homicide unit also requires support from specialized intelligence units, an efficient crime lab, productive coordination with prosecutors, effective training programs, and many other elements to produce success. Many agencies have applied community policing strategies to homicide investigations, knowing that residents' trust in law enforcement fosters a greater willingness to cooperate with officers during an investigation.

Because neither the law enforcement nor prosecutorial processes are perfect, there must always be concern that wrongful convictions can occur. In fact, one of the most significant developments in criminal justice during recent decades has been the growing understanding of how fallible the U.S. justice system is, as new technologies, DNA evidence in particular, have exonerated many people who had been convicted and sentenced to long prison terms or even to death. To prevent this, law enforcement administrators must consider an ever-growing number of policy options, scientific protocols, and legal safeguards. The challenge for law enforcement and prosecutors is to make sense of this ever-increasing complexity while preventing wrongful convictions.

PROMOTING EFFECTIVE HOMICIDE INVESTIGATIONS CONFERENCE

The "Promoting Effective Homicide Investigations" conference, held May 25–26, 2006 in Washington, D.C., and sponsored by the Office of Community Oriented Policing Services (the COPS Office), served as the foundation for this publication. PERF invited more than 100 law enforcement and related personnel, including chiefs, commanders, detectives, crime scene personnel, crime analysts, prosecutors, and defense attorneys, to discuss dynamic and successful approaches to homicide investigations. The meeting served as the basis for identifying and examining the ways that law enforcement agencies work to increase clearance rates while preventing wrongful convictions, including videotaping interrogations, suspect lineups, photo arrays, DNA collection and analysis, and cold case squads.

REPORT CONTENTS

This publication, which is intended to help agency executives, administrators, investigators, and prosecutors increase the effectiveness of homicide investigations, focuses on the policy options, scientific protocols, and legal safeguards confronting law enforcement executives. It includes lessons learned and challenges faced as well as success stories from agencies with experience implementing these policies. The contents are based on information gathered from conference participants, along with data collected during site visits at selected departments and interviews conducted by PERF staff with law enforcement professionals and other interested parties throughout 2006. Examples of policies for homicide units, cold case squads, and other materials are included in the appendixes.

Several themes emerge from this publication. First, there is no perfect formula for preventing and/or solving homicides, but a number of remarkable initiatives and promising practices have helped agencies in their investigations. Second, despite the differences among law enforcement agencies, many face the same problems when dealing with an increasing crime rate and a reduction in clearance rates. Law enforcement administrators can find valuable assistance in the experiences of a neighboring agency, or in the determination of a particular investigator to solve problems and get things done. Departments should evaluate their needs, resources, and capabilities in all areas to determine which approaches are most beneficial to them. As homicide rates rise in many places around the country and clearance rates decrease, the information in this publication will give police executives and investigators a starting point for developing policies and practices to increase overall investigative effectiveness.

2

Homicides and Clearance Rates

ACCORDING TO THE FEDERAL BUREAU OF INVESTIGATION'S (FBI) Annual Uniform Crime Reports (UCR) for 2005, the number of homicides in the United States increased by 4.8 percent compared to 2004—the largest single-year increase for homicides in 14 years. And, for June 2006 the trend continued, with preliminary UCR data showing that homicide increased by 0.3 percent, with a much larger increase of 6.7 percent in cities with populations of 1 million or more.

While the number of homicides in the U.S. has fluctuated since the 1960s, the number of homicides being *solved* has decreased in that time. Homicide clearance rates have decreased by approximately 30 percent since the 1960s. Despite this overall national decrease, however, some jurisdictions have maintained their ability to solve homicides at a high rate.

This chapter provides an overview of homicide rates and clearance rates in the United States. It discusses the effect of unsolved homicides on the department and the community. This chapter also highlights trends affecting homicide investigations and investigative factors associated with cleared homicide cases. Strategies for improving homicide clearance rates are examined, as well.

OVERVIEW OF HOMICIDE RATES AND CLEARANCE RATES

Since 1930, the FBI has annually collected data on the number of crimes reported from more than 17,000 law enforcement agencies in the United

States and the number of crimes that are cleared by an arrest. The FBI releases this information to the public through its UCRs. For the purposes of the UCR, a crime is considered cleared if at least one person has been 1. arrested, 2. charged with the crime, and 3. handed over to the courts for prosecution.[1]

The UCR also considers some cases cleared when certain "exceptional means" are met. For a case to be cleared by "exceptional means," the law enforcement agency must have identified the offender; gathered enough evidence to make an arrest, charge the offender, and turn him over for prosecution; identified the offender's exact location; and encountered some circumstance beyond the agency's control that prevented it from making an arrest. An example of a homicide cleared by "exceptional means" would be a homicide/suicide. Self-defense homicides also are considered cleared by "exceptional means."

The homicide clearance rate is determined by dividing the total number of homicides reported in a year by the number of arrests and "exceptional means" homicides. For the purpose of this report, the terms "cleared," "closed," and "solved" will be used interchangeably.

The UCR homicide clearance rate is also affected by solved cold case homicides (homicides that occurred in previous years but were solved during current reporting years). In some years, some agencies might have a clearance rate greater than 100 percent. If a homicide committed in 1992 was solved in 2004, for example, the 2004 homicide clearance rate would be artificially high because the homicide was not reported in 2004 but was included as a cleared case in 2004. Conversely, if a death from a previous year is ruled a homicide in the current year it counts as a current year murder.

Homicide Rates 1961–2005

Figure 1 shows the number of homicides reported by law enforcement agencies in the United States from 1961 to 2005. It shows an increase in homicides from the 1960s to the early to mid-1990s. In 1993, 24,526 homicides were reported in the U.S., but by 2004 that number dropped to 16,137. In 2005, a 3.4 percent increase in the number of homicides,

---

[1]. *Uniform Crime Reporting Handbook,* Washington, D.C.: U.S. Department of Justice, Federal Bureau of Investigation, 2004. http://www.fbi.gov/ucr/handbook/ucrhandbook04.pdf

Cleared by Exceptional Means. In certain situations, law enforcement is not able to satisfy the three conditions necessary to clear a homicide by arrest. Yet if agencies can answer all of the following questions in the affirmative, they can clear the offense *exceptionally* for the purpose of reporting to the UCR.

1. Has the investigation definitely established the identity of the offender?
2. Is there enough information to support an arrest, charge, and to turn over to the court for prosecution?
3. Is the exact location of the offender known so that the subject could be taken into custody now?
4. Is there some reason outside law enforcement control that precludes arresting, charging, and prosecuting the offender?

Examples of Exceptional Clearances. Generally, an offense can be exceptionally cleared when it falls into one of the following categories. The list is not all-inclusive; there may be other circumstances in which a law enforcement agency is entitled to an exceptional clearance.

1. Suicide of the offender. (The person who committed the offense is dead.)
2. Double homicide. (Two persons kill each other.)
3. Deathbed confession. (The person who committed the offense dies after making the confession.)
4. Offender killed by police or citizen.
5. Confession by an offender who is already in law enforcement custody or serving a sentence. (This is actually a variation of a true

---

2. *Ibid.*

clearance by arrest—the offender would not be "apprehended" but in most situations would be prosecuted on the new charge.)

6. Offender is prosecuted by state or local authorities in another city for a different offense or is prosecuted in another city or state by the Federal Government for an offense that may be the same. (Law enforcement makes an attempt to obtain the return of the offender for prosecution, but the other jurisdiction will not allow the release.)

7. Extradition denied.

8. Victim refuses to cooperate in the prosecution. (This action alone does not unfound the offense. The answer must also be *yes* to questions 1, 2, and 3 in the section Cleared by Exceptional Means.)

9. Warrant is outstanding for felon but before being arrested the offender dies. (The method of death is irrelevant.)

10. The handling of a juvenile offender either orally or by written notice to parents in instances involving minor offenses such as petty larceny, and no referral is made to juvenile court as a matter of publicly accepted law enforcement policy.

The UCR recognizes that departmental policy in various law enforcement agencies permits discontinuing an investigation and administratively closing cases for which all investigation has been completed. The administrative closing of a case or the clearing of it by departmental policy does not permit exceptionally clearing the offense for UCR unless all four questions mentioned earlier can be answered *yes*. Additionally, the recovery of property does not clear a case. Clearances in accordance with UCR procedures should have no effect on whether an agency has internal policies for closing a case or discontinuing an active investigation. ■

compared to 2004, indicated that the downward trend may be ending. The preliminary data for 2006 show a continued increase in the number of homicides.

The number of homicides experienced by individual jurisdictions does not necessarily follow the national trend depicted in Figure 1. Some jurisdictions have seen a decrease greater than the national average during the late 1990s, while other jurisdictions have experienced an increase in reported homicides.

Figure 2 controls for the increase in the U.S. population, showing the homicide rate per 100,000 inhabitants from 1961 to 2005. This figure indicates that the current homicide rate per 100,000 inhabitants is close

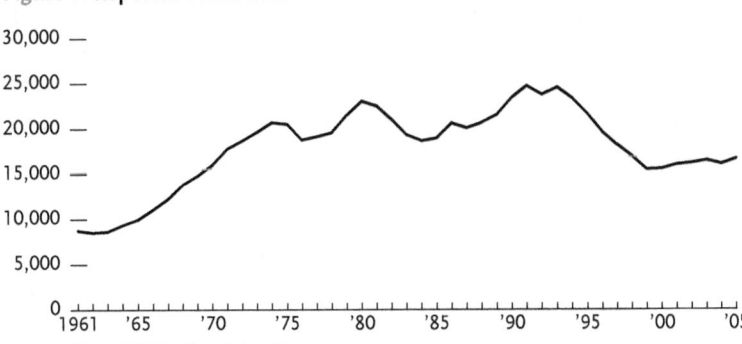

Figure 1. **Reported Homicides in U.S. from 1961 to 2005**

Source of Data: FBI Uniform Crime Reports

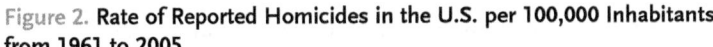

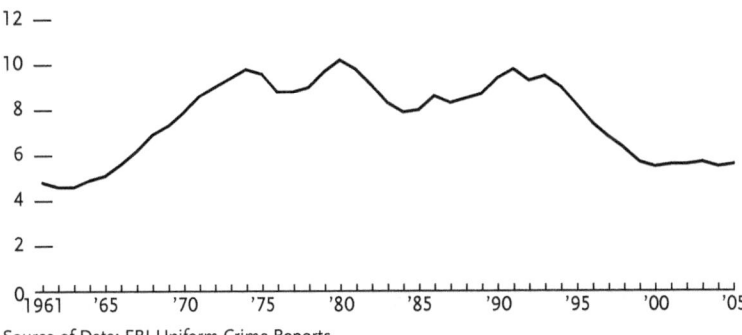

Figure 2. **Rate of Reported Homicides in the U.S. per 100,000 Inhabitants from 1961 to 2005**

Source of Data: FBI Uniform Crime Reports

to the homicide rates of the 1960s. During the 1960s there were approximately 5 homicides for every 100,000 people in the U.S. In 2005, the homicide rate per 100,000 inhabitants was 5.6, a figure that is 0.1 higher than in 2004. Similar to Figure 1, this figure indicates a decrease in the homicide rate beginning in 1994.

Clearance Rates 1961–2005

Figure 3 depicts the homicide clearance rates in the U.S. from 1961 to 2005. An arrest was made or homicides were otherwise cleared in 92 percent of the cases in 1961 and only 61 percent of homicides in 2005. While the national homicide clearance rate for the U.S. has fallen, the homicide clearance rates for some individual jurisdictions have consistently remained above the falling national rate. Cities such as Dallas, Milwaukee, and San Jose have historically had higher homicide clearance rates than the national average, while other cities have had consistently lower homicide clearance rates than the national average. There is some debate over using clearance rates as a measure of law enforcement performance (see Chapter 3 for additional information on performance). While the arrest of a suspect is an important step in the investigative process, little attention is paid to how many of those arrests result in convictions. Yet clearance rates are often defined as the arrest of the most probable crime suspect.

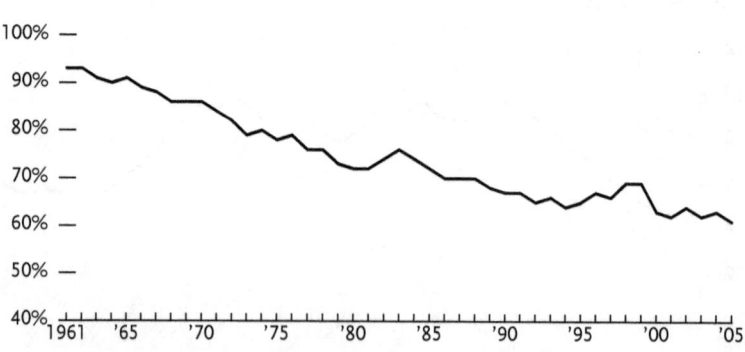

Figure 3. **Homicide Clearance Rates in the U.S. from 1961 to 2005**

Source of Data: FBI Uniform Crime Reports

CHANGING TRENDS IN THE NATURE OF HOMICIDES

Traditionally and typically, homicides have been crimes of passion committed by family members or close acquaintances. The relationship between the offender and victim and the circumstances surrounding the homicide made the crimes easier for law enforcement to solve. These types of homicides (referred to as "acquaintance homicides") generally result from an argument and are frequently unplanned. Witnesses are more likely to hear or see something in these cases. And in many acquaintance homicides the offender is more likely to surrender to law enforcement because of feelings of guilt.[3] In recent years, however, the number of homicides involving strangers has grown. This has been attributed to an increase in drug activity and firearms possession among youth. A study examining homicide trends in San Diego from 1970 to 1980 identified a doubling of the "stranger homicide" category, from 33 percent of all homicides in 1970 to 66 percent in 1980.[4]

Stranger homicides are more difficult to solve. For one thing, it is more difficult to determine the motivation for the crime. Second, it is more difficult to identify suspects simply because the pool of suspects in stranger homicides is larger than in acquaintance homicides.

Variables Affecting Law Enforcement's Investigation of Homicide Cases

Several major variables have emerged that hamper the ability of departments to investigate and solve homicides. These variables include offender reentry, illegal immigrants as reluctant witnesses, witness intimidation and noncooperation, and the influences of "thug culture" on communities.

Offender Reentry

Across the country large numbers of prisoners are being released to communities—about 650,000 per year, according to the U.S. Department

---

[3]. Richardson, D., and R. Kosa. *An Examination of Homicide Clearance Rates: Foundation for the Development of a Homicide Clearance Model.* 2001. http://www.policeforum.org/upload/Homicide%20Clearance%20Rates%20-%20Model_576683258_1229200516132.pdf

[4]. Gilbert, J.N. (1983). "A Study of the Increased Rate of Unsolved Criminal Homicides in San Diego, CA, and Its Relationship to Police Investigative Effectiveness." *American Journal of Police: An Interdisciplinary Journal of Theory and Research* 2 (1983), 149–166.

of Justice, and a significant number are returning to the country's population centers—large cities and densely populated counties. They return with problems such as poor health and poor prospects for employment that make their assimilation into society difficult. Many released prisoners revert back to criminal activity, including violent crime, as they try to settle old vendettas or establish a criminal enterprise on someone else's turf. In some cases, their mere presence creates fear in community residents. According to a recent COPS Office report, "Roughly two-thirds of released prisoners are rearrested within three years of release; nearly half of all releasees return to prison within the same period, either for a new crime or for a technical violation of the conditions of their release."[5]

Illegal Immigrants as Reluctant Witnesses

The growing diversity in the United States and the increase in illegal immigration have also affected law enforcement's ability to investigate homicides. In some immigrant communities gangs such as MS 13, whose members have strong ties to recent immigrants, prey on these people. Immigrants from certain countries may fear police officers, based on their interaction with law enforcement in their country of origin, making them reluctant to cooperate during an investigation. Additionally, illegal immigrants who witness a homicide may be reluctant to come forward for fear of deportation. In cases where immigrants do come forward, law enforcement agencies often lack the skills necessary to work with minority communities—both in interpreting and having an awareness of cultural differences. This problem may worsen as illegal immigration becomes a major political issue, and Congress may increase immigration enforcement measures while local communities consider laws or policies requiring local law enforcement to inquire about the legal status of those they encounter.

Thug Culture

The growth of a "thug culture" (or "oppositional culture"), especially in America's inner cities, has also had an impact on the ability of law

---

5. LaVigne, Nancy G., Amy L. Solomon, Karen A. Beckman, and Kelly Dedel. *Prisoner Reentry and Community Policing: Strategies for Enhancing Public Safety*. Washington, D.C.: Urban Institute, 2006, p. 8.

enforcement to investigate homicides. The term "thug culture" refers to community members who reject the values and aspirations of mainstream society. Thug culture members typically gain respect through violence.[6] For example, in 2004, a DVD titled "Stop Snitchin'" surfaced in Baltimore, depicting drug dealers complaining about former associates who had cooperated with law enforcement. A well-known National Basketball Association player was also featured in the DVD. The DVD soon became an underground hit that led to "Stop Snitchin'" T-shirts, which became popular among hip-hop artists who helped spread the message across the country.

Witness Intimidation

Lower socioeconomic neighborhoods are greatly affected by local gangs, whose members tend to see violence as a reasonable response to resolving conflicts. Gang members often intimidate witnesses into not cooperating with law enforcement. Cities such as Baltimore and Boston have had several recent cases where witnesses have been killed for cooperating with law enforcement.

Consequences of Unsolved Homicides

Unsolved homicides hamper the healing process for the family and friends of the victim, and have a significant effect on communities and all aspects of the criminal justice system. In addition to affecting the criminal justice system's ability to deter crime, reduced clearance rates may lower the public's confidence in the police, increase fear in the community, and affect officer performance. Of course, the most important consequence of an unsolved homicide is that a killer remains free, able to commit additional murders or become a victim himself.

Deterrence

The decrease in arrests for homicides over time means there has been a decrease in the effectiveness of the criminal justice system to hold homicide offenders accountable. This, in turn, can lead to a decrease in both

---

6. Sherman, L., D. Gottfredson, D. MacKenzie, J. Eck, P. Reuter, and S. Bushway. *Preventing Crime: What Works, What Doesn't, What's Promising.* A Report to the United States Congress. Washington, D.C.: National Institute of Justice, 1997. http://www.ncjrs.gov/works/

the *general* and *specific* deterrent effect of punishment.[7] Under the specific deterrence theory, offenders who are arrested and punished are less likely to commit new crimes because they do not want to be punished again. The general deterrence theory holds that the threat of apprehension and punishment deters people generally from committing crimes in the first place. To the extent that offenders literally "get away with murder" and the public knows about it, both types of deterrence can be expected to diminish.

Officer Performance

Unsolved homicides can have an impact on the productivity of a homicide investigator. New cases are assigned to the officer, decreasing the amount of time an officer has to spend on the unsolved case. Additionally, unsolved homicides can affect the entire department. With an increase in the number of unsolved homicides, a department may have to reallocate additional resources to the homicide unit to assist in solving cases, thereby reducing resources in another area.

Public Fear

Unsolved homicides can reduce the public's confidence in the ability of officers to do their job and can lead to an increase in the level of fear in the community. This lack of confidence and increased fear can make residents reluctant to come forward and cooperate with the police. The lack of cooperation affects the investigator's ability to solve cases, which contributes to an increase in unsolved cases, completing the vicious circle. Fear is further heightened in communities with gangs who are known to intimidate witnesses to prevent them from cooperating with law enforcement.[8]

The Effects on Families and Friends

An unsolved homicide also affects the victim's family members and friends, increasing their sadness, frustration, and anger. In addition to

---

[7]. Beccaria, C. *On Crimes and Punishment*. Translated by H. Paolucci. (Original work published in 1764). New York: Bobbs-Merrill Co., Inc., 1963.

[8]. Finn, P. and K.M. Healey. (1996). *Preventing Gang- and Drug-Related Witness Intimidation*. Washington, D.C.: National Institute of Justice, Issues and Practices, NCJ 163067, November 1996. http://www.ncjrs.gov/pdffiles/163067.pdf

being upset about the death and angry with the perpetrator, family members may become upset with the police if an arrest is not made, especially if they believe that the police have failed to work hard enough on the case. This may make them less likely to cooperate with law enforcement in the future. Additionally, children who witness a homicide may suffer psychological damage, such as becoming extremely fearful of additional violent acts to their family, friends, and even themselves.[9]

CONSIDERATIONS FOR LAW ENFORCEMENT AGENCIES

Law enforcement executives should be cognizant of a number of issues regarding homicide clearance rates. Each of these issues is explored in more detail in subsequent chapters. The first consideration is whether an agency should have a centralized or decentralized homicide unit. Some officials argue that decentralized units allow investigators to work more closely with residents and patrol officers assigned to neighborhoods and that, in turn, helps with identifying witnesses and informants and generally improves the flow of information to investigators. Others argue that a decentralized model has costs in terms of loss of efficiency and investigative expertise that offset any benefits gained from decentralization (see Chapter 3 for an additional discussion of decentralization). At this point, limited research has been conducted into the efficiency and effectiveness of the different models, so departments need to consider which arrangement best fits their needs and resources.

The second consideration for law enforcement executives is the positive effect of cold case squads on homicide clearance rates. Cold case squads review older unsolved homicide cases to determine if there is a possibility of clearing the case. If the case is deemed solvable after reviewing the homicide file, the cold case squad begins an investigation. (See Chapter 7 for more information on cold case units.)

Closely related to cold case units is the third area affecting homicide clearance rates, the use of DNA evidence. Recent advances in technology now make it possible to link small amounts of DNA evidence found at a

---

9. Stiles, M. "Witnessing Domestic Violence: The Effect on Children." *American Family Physician* 66/11, December 1, 2002. http://www.aafp.org/afp/20021201/medicine.html

crime scene with suspected offenders. Some police departments have received federal funding to examine DNA evidence. For example, the Kansas City, Missouri, Police Department was awarded a $100,000 federal grant to examine DNA evidence. This, in conjunction with the work by its cold case squad, has led to an increase in its homicide clearance rates. (See Chapter 6 for more information on DNA.)

Other areas that law enforcement executives should consider that may affect their ability to make an arrest in a homicide case and are helpful during prosecution include: eyewitness identification techniques (Chapter 4); videotaping interrogations (Chapter 5); and the police department's working relationship with, and authority over, the crime lab (Chapter 6).

CONCLUSION

The practices and procedures of a police department and its individual officers *can* affect the department's homicide clearance rate. The national clearance rate for homicides in the United States has been declining since the 1960s, but during that time some police departments have maintained consistently high clearance rates. Police executives should examine the policies of those departments with consistently high clearance rates to determine whether they have implications for improving their own homicide clearance rates.

3

Managing Homicide Units for Effectiveness

THE INVESTIGATION OF A HOMICIDE IS ONE OF THE MOST critical responsibilities of any local law enforcement agency. Police chiefs and homicide commanders often are judged by the number of homicides that occur in their jurisdictions and by their ability to clear cases. The FBI's annual Uniform Crime Report highlights violent crime, including the number of homicides in each jurisdiction. The news media routinely use such data to determine whether a city is safe or dangerous[1] and to make overall, but simplistic, judgments about the quality of life of various cities. Residents react to increased homicides and large numbers of unsolved homicides with great concern, and sometimes indicate that their confidence in a law enforcement agency is affected by these rates.

This chapter focuses on some of the management and personnel policies of homicide units that agency administrators should consider when examining effectiveness. The first section of this chapter presents an overview of the organizational characteristics of homicide units. The second section discusses the influence of organizational characteristics on clearance rates and effectiveness, using research findings and current practices to illustrate the role that policies and procedures play in making a homicide unit effective.

---

1. Morgan Quitno Press, Lawrence, Kansas, publishes one such annual list: *City Crime Rankings*. http://www.morganquitno.com

ORGANIZATIONAL CHARACTERISTICS

Homicide units, like police departments, vary significantly in size and responsibilities. Table 1 presents an overview of several homicide units, including personnel assigned to the units and several other indicators that highlight differences.

As can be seen in Table 1, departments serving cities with similar populations do not always have similar numbers of personnel. The number of detectives in a homicide unit and the number of cases assigned to those detectives vary significantly. A detective in Seattle may have a caseload of only one homicide while a detective in Detroit may carry a caseload of 10 homicides.

Table 1. **Homicide Unit Characteristics by Demographic Variables**

Police agency	City pop.	Sworn personnel NUM.	PER 1,000 RESIDENTS	Homicide detectives NUM.	PER 100 SWORN PERSONNEL	2004 homicides NUM.	PER HOMICIDE DETECTIVE	CLEARANCE RATE
Houston	1,953,631	4,905	2.51	62	1.26	272	4.38	59.6%
Las Vegas Metro	1,800,100	3,200	1.88	24	0.75	138	5.75	54.2%
San Jose	904,522	1,354	1.41	11	0.81	24	2.18	83.3%
Detroit	900,198	3,252	3.75	39	1.19	383	9.82	37.4%
Memphis	678,988	2,087	3.32	24	0.76	107	6.68	80%
Baltimore	609,779	3,200	5.24	48	2.50	276	3.45	59.4%
Seattle	571,480	1,280	2.23	19	1.79	24	1.04	70.8%
Boston	569,165	1,900	3.62	20	1.05	61	3.05	27.9%
Washington D.C. Metro	557,598	3,615	6.97	73	1.16	198	4.71	60.6%
Kansas City, MO	441,545	1,289	2.89	22	1.70	87	3.95	63%
Oakland	399,484	700	1.91	13	1.85	88	6.76	34.9%

The numbers in this chart must be considered in light of dozens of factors or conditions that exist in one city but not another. The concentration of poverty, the level of education, the population density, or a city's square mileage can influence these numbers. The type of crime can influence the numbers, as well. A city with a high rate of domestic violence might have a higher clearance rate than a city with a high rate of gang violence. Other factors, such as witness cooperation or the existence of a witness protection program can influence the homicide and homicide clearance rates.

Although comparing agency attributes is an interesting exercise, it does not provide much guidance for managers to consider when examining their own homicide units. Rather, managers have to carefully examine the goals and resources of their own agency to determine the appropriate staffing levels and caseloads for investigators. Agencies should develop and periodically evaluate measures of workload and effectiveness for investigators.[2]

Responsibilities of the Homicide Unit

Many factors must be taken into account when comparing homicide units, police departments, and clearance rates. In many cases, the responsibilities of units can be quite different, with many units being responsible for investigating other matters in addition to homicides. Some of the other crimes investigated by a homicide unit can include: in-custody deaths, suicides, serious injuries to prisoners, accidental deaths, aggravated assaults with weapons, officer-involved shootings, kidnappings, cold cases, and industrial accidents with life-threatening injury.

Some homicide units are responsible for investigating shootings, stabbings and other serious assaults where the victim did not die. Some refer to these incidents as failed homicides, and attribute the failure to the availability of medical trauma centers and advances in emergency medical care. The Detroit Police Department homicide unit, for example, now takes responsibility for a case if the assault victim is listed in

---

2. Williams, Gerald L. "Criminal Investigations," in *Local Government Police Management*, International City/County Management Association, Washington, D.C.: 2003.

critical condition. The Kansas City, Missouri, and Boston homicide units also investigate attempted homicides, while the Seattle Police Department has consolidated the investigations of assaults and homicides into one unit.

Another area of responsibility for some homicide units is officer-involved shootings. Some units respond only if a suspect is shot, while others respond to any scene where an officer intentionally discharged a firearm. A few agencies, including the Los Angeles Police Department and the Washington, D.C., Metropolitan Police Department, have created special units apart from homicide units to investigate officer-involved shootings and other use-of-force investigations, which allow homicide units to focus their time and resources solely on homicides. In some agencies, depending on the circumstances of the shooting, an internal affairs unit may investigate the shooting to determine whether the shooting is consistent with agency policies.

Centralization versus Decentralization

Some large police departments have decentralized some or all of their detective functions by moving investigators from a central location (e.g., headquarters) to districts and assigning them to specific geographic locations.[3] Community policing, which emphasizes decentralization as a means of improving relations with residents and increasing trust, has been the primary motivation in this decision. It would follow, therefore, that decentralized investigative units should be more effective because of a greater understanding of area crime patterns and a better working relationship with the people who live and work there.

For some departments, the trend toward decentralization has included homicide units. Professor Charles Wellford of the University of Maryland stated, "The logic of community policing, as it is applied to a homicide investigation situation, suggests to me decentralization can help overcome the reluctance of community members to assist police—provided that the level of morale and prestige that comes with

---

3. Wycoff, Mary Ann. *Investigations in the Community Policing Context.* Washington, D.C.: Police Executive Research Forum, 2001.

participation in a central unit can be maintained by the department. That is a big 'IF' and one that needs careful consideration."[4]

Furthermore, while decentralization provides significant advantages for some investigative units, it may not provide those same advantages for all units. Anecdotally, a number of large departments have found that decentralization of major crime investigative units, such as robbery and homicide, does not increase productivity. Several years ago, the Washington, D.C., Metropolitan Police Department decentralized its homicide unit, but because the results were mixed, Chief Charles Ramsey reevaluated his decision and centralized the unit, in part because decentralization diluted the pool of talented homicide investigators and supervisors, making them less effective.

According to experienced law enforcement officials, the complexity of both the crime of homicide and the investigation of homicides requires some form of centralization.[5] Some very large police departments have homicide detectives in districts, but also maintain a centralized homicide unit for high-profile or more complex cases. In the New York City Police Department, for example, precinct detectives are responsible for homicides within their precinct; however, homicide detectives from the centralized unit can respond to assist precinct detectives and play a supporting role during investigations. Ultimately, the most effective arrangement may be based on the factors specific to a particular jurisdiction, depending on workload, jurisdiction size, expertise, training, and the responsibilities of the homicide unit.

The paucity of research into organizational characteristics makes it difficult to draw definitive conclusions about the most effective arrangement, although Wellford, in his groundbreaking research into clearance rates, found that decentralized homicide units had lower clearance rates than centralized units.[6] The next section of the chapter

---

4. Wellford, C. *Oversight Report on the Metropolitan Police Department Homicide Investigative Practices and Case Closure Rate*. Committee on the Judiciary, Washington D.C., City Council, February 27, 2001. http://www.dcwatch.com/police/010227.htm
5. Wellford, C. "Improving Homicide Clearance Rates," in *National Community Policing Conference, July 27–29, 2006*. Washington, D.C.: U.S. Department of Justice, Office of Community Oriented Policing Services.
6. Wellford, C. and J. Cronin. *Homicides: What Police Can Do to Improve Clearance Rates*. Washington, D.C.: National Institute of Justice, April 2–7, 2000.

discusses inmore detail the findings of Wellford's work and compares it to how departments organize their homicide units.

VARIABLES AFFECTING HOMICIDE CLEARANCE RATES

Surprisingly, very little research has been conducted into how police policies, procedures, and tactics influence the effectiveness of homicide investigations. There has been speculation surrounding the factors associated with solving a homicide case but almost no systematic examination of these issues. The only study known to empirically examine police investigations of homicides was conducted by researchers from the University of Maryland, working in conjunction with the Justice Research and Statistics Association.[7] The authors concluded that certain actions taken by police *can* have a statistically significant impact on solving a homicide.

In 2000, the researchers examined the homicide clearance rates of 20 major U.S. cities and determined that, for the most part, a given city's homicide clearance rate remained relatively stable over time. To examine this finding further, the researchers collected data on approximately 200 homicide cases from each of four cities: two with traditionally high homicide clearance rates and two with traditionally low clearance rates. To encourage participation, the researchers agreed not to reveal the identity of the cities chosen for their study. They examined case characteristics, such as location of the homicide, characteristics of the offender and victim, type of weapon used, and drug involvement in the homicide. They also examined police practices and procedures, such as: number of minutes taken for the detective to arrive at the scene; number of detectives assigned to the case; whether a neighborhood canvas was conducted; whether criminal computer checks were conducted on the victim, the suspect and witnesses; the extent to which confidential informants were used; and actions taken by the first officer(s) on the scene.

The researchers grouped these variables into three categories: 1. initial response, 2. actions of the detectives, and 3. other police responses. The focus of this section of the chapter is to highlight the

---

7. *Ibid.*

variables that are within the control of law enforcement, identified by researchers as having a positive effect on the clearance of a homicide. Along with the variables are examples of agency policies and practices that increase clearance rates.

Initial Response

The following are the variables associated with successfully clearing a homicide case during the initial response:

- The first officer on the scene immediately notifies the homicide unit, the medical examiner's office, and the crime lab.
- The first officer on the scene immediately secures the area and attempts to locate witnesses.
- The detective assigned to the case arrives at the scene within 30 minutes of being notified.

The quality of the initial investigation—which includes the actions of the responding officer(s)—is crucial to the success of the entire investigation. Actions taken by the first officer to arrive at the crime scene, such as preserving the scene and evidence, contribute to solving the homicide. Based on these findings, law enforcement agencies should make patrol officers aware of their impact on the investigation and ensure that they receive proper training as the first officer to respond to a homicide scene. Some departments rely on roll-call training to teach patrol officers how to better handle crime scenes, including identifying potential witnesses. This sort of training is critical, given that patrol officers are almost always the first to arrive at homicide scenes. Additionally, the speed with which detectives arrive at the crime scene affects their ability to ensure that the crime scene is processed properly and quickly.

Actions of the Detectives

The variables in the "actions of the detectives" category that were associated with solving a case include the following:

- Three or four detectives, instead of one or two, were assigned to the case.

- The detectives took detailed notes describing the crime scene, including measurements.
- Detectives followed up on all information provide by witnesses.
- At least one detective assigned to the case attended the postmortem examination.

Attention to detail by investigators is crucial. Solved homicide cases are more likely to have been investigated by detectives who performed the actions listed above. Law enforcement agencies should keep this information in mind when selecting and training homicide detectives. Another priority is to ensure that a sufficient number of detectives is available to follow through with all aspects of the case.

Many departments assign a primary team of two homicide detectives to an investigation. Some departments have supervisors respond to the scene, but others, especially those with larger numbers of homicides, do not. Crime scene specialists, whether police officers or civilians, also respond to every scene. Many departments seem to have good working relationships between investigators and crime scene specialists. Others, however, indicate that coordination between investigators and forensic specialists could be improved through clearer delineation of roles and responsibilities, coupled with an emphasis on understanding the different perspectives each position brings to the investigation. Departments should have clear written policies on the collection and preservation of physical evidence.

Although homicide detectives tend to be highly motivated individuals, the complexity of the work requires a certain level of supervisory review, and in some cases, outside review. In addition to direct supervision and oversight, some agencies rely on systems of internal and/or external review of homicide investigations.

Most units come together to "brainstorm" either early in an investigation or on a weekly or monthly basis. The amount of time spent openly discussing the cases seems to depend on the volume of cases. One unit commander stated that the volume of cases in his department is just too high to devote time to unit meetings, so his detectives discuss cases more informally. Whether cases are discussed formally or informally, it is important that other detectives in the unit are regularly briefed and given the opportunity to ask questions. These discussions tend to foster a team environment and can lead to valuable input.

Other Police Actions

The variables in the "other police responses" category that were found to increase the likelihood that a homicide would be solved include the following:

- A computer check using the local criminal justice information system was conducted on the suspect or on any guns found.
- A witness interviewed at the crime scene provided valuable evidence, such as information about circumstances of the death or the perpetrator's motivation, an identification of the suspect or victim, or the whereabouts of the suspect.
- Witnesses, friends, acquaintances, and neighbors of the victim were interviewed.
- The medical examiner prepared a body chart of the victim and it was included in the case file.
- The attending physician and medical personnel were interviewed.
- Confidential informants provided information.

The actions taken by police officers *do* have an impact on solving homicides; however, there is no guarantee that a homicide will be cleared if the investigating officers complete all the steps identified by the researchers. Every homicide case begins with a different level of solvability and a different probability of arrests. Some cases are easier to solve (for example, those in which the offender is still at the crime scene when officers arrive), while others are more difficult or almost impossible to solve (such as those where there are no witnesses, no evidence, and no suspect can be identified). Nevertheless, if officers follow certain procedures during the investigation, the likelihood of clearing the homicide can increase.

A law enforcement agency's ability to gain and maintain witness cooperation in an investigation is also crucial to solving homicides. The two primary facets on which a department should focus regarding witness cooperation are 1. improving police-community relations before homicides occur, and 2. protecting witnesses from intimidation. Some witnesses are reluctant to come forward because of a fear of retaliation; others are reluctant because of a distrust of the police and the criminal justice system. Witness cooperation is paramount to homicide investigations and every effort should be made by a department to foster that cooperation through community policing.

Personnel Policies

Agencies can examine a number of personnel policies and practices that could influence the effectiveness of homicide investigations. Some personnel policies may contribute to high homicide clearance rates.

- Homicide unit supervisors can select the best detectives from other units.

- Homicide investigators do not regularly rotate out of the unit, but are allowed to stay and gain expertise.

- Homicide detectives are given latitude to work on a case while on overtime.

- Investigators are assigned cars on a 24-hour basis, allowing them to respond directly to a crime scene instead of having to report to headquarters to sign out a car.

Selection and Training of Investigators

The selection and training of homicide investigators is critical to the success of homicide investigations. Yet the selection methods and training programs vary greatly by agency, and can be influenced by factors such as organizational tradition, labor agreements, transfer policies, and supervisory preference.

A common approach to selecting homicide detectives is to handpick them from other investigative units, particularly robbery, narcotics, and gang units. Many homicides involve gang connections and/or narcotics; therefore, the ability to communicate with and understand the culture of gang members can be valuable to a homicide unit. Another approach to selecting detectives involves a formal selection process that can include a combination of written exams and oral interviews.

Once selected for assignment to a homicide unit, detectives may undergo specialized training. For some it may be a simple investigator's course; for others it may be a homicide investigator's course that includes topics such as interview and interrogation, and preparation and service of search warrants and wiretaps. In addition to classroom training, most investigators receive on-the-job training. Further, some departments have developed a field training program in which unit commanders attempt to pair seasoned investigators with more junior detectives. Agencies should ensure that investigators have proper training, especially in the areas of current case law and interview and interrogation. In-service or ongoing training for investigators is crucial for keeping them informed of changing procedures or advances in areas such as forensic sciences.

Rotation Policies

Another critical and sometimes contentious issue in homicide units is the duration of assignment in the unit. Many argue that allowing detectives to stay in the unit indefinitely allows them to gain valuable experience and expertise, such as becoming an adept interrogator. Rotating detectives out of the homicide unit can deplete investigative expertise and make it difficult to provide on-the-job training to new investigators. Others argue that a regular rotation policy benefits organizational and individual officers' career development. As officers transfer to other units, investigative expertise is distributed throughout the entire department. Chiefs must carefully consider the overall goals for organizational and career development, as well as any labor agreements, when determining the most appropriate rotation policy for officers in homicide units. Proper training programs for new investigators should accompany mandatory rotation policies.

Investigator Schedules and Overtime

The schedule of a homicide investigator should be consistent with the case workload and the temporal distribution of homicides. In some departments, homicide detectives work regular business hours, Monday though Friday. In others, detectives work shifts to provide coverage 24

One Department's Approach
by Robert L. Davis, Chief of Police,
San Jose (California) Police Department

I attribute the 90 percent case clearance rate of the San Jose Police Department's Homicide Unit to three main factors:

1. The San Jose Police Department (SJPD) has a *mandatory rotation policy* for its officers and sergeants, which limits the time they can serve in a specialized assignment before returning to patrol for at least 1 year. In the case of the Homicide Unit, officers may serve for 5 years and sergeants for 6 years before being required to return to patrol. This policy ensures that the department is composed of patrol officers who are also highly trained investigators. Literally hundreds of SJPD patrol officers, sergeants, and commanders have served as detectives in a variety of investigative units during their careers. It is not unusual that the first responders at a homicide crime scene are patrol officers with a background in homicide investigations or crime scene processing. Their expertise in handling the important preliminary investigation in the field gives a head start to the homicide unit detectives when they arrive on-scene.

    Moreover, this rotation policy provides opportunities for officers at the beginning of their career to be trained to conduct investigations. The enthusiasm of the younger investigators has energized some of the department's senior detectives in every unit, and their fresh look at unsolved homicides has led to the clearance of some of these cases.

2. Solving a homicide case frequently depends on *community support and witness cooperation*. It is extremely important that such information be provided within the first few hours of a case. The SJPD,

serving a city of nearly one million people, has gone to great lengths to establish a trusting relationship with the many different racial and ethnic groups that reside in the city. The department has solved homicide cases because residents have been willing to come forward and share key pieces of information. Many do so knowing that the department will go out of its way to accommodate those who want to remain anonymous. Those who are here illegally do not have to fear for their immigration status if they choose to come forward with information about a crime. The importance of this level of community support and mutual trust cannot be overstated when discussing the homicide clearance rate.

3. It is imperative that those chosen to serve in the homicide unit are provided the *training and networking opportunities* to help them develop investigative skills. This includes training in interviewing and interrogating, as well as attending professional gatherings of other homicide investigators. While the training can be expensive, particularly the amount of time detectives need to be away, it is a priority for our department. Great investigations require great investigators, and training is always a wise investment in officers. ■

hours a day, 7 days a week. Other agencies meet the workload demands by rotating detectives on evening and weekend shifts. Another arrangement that many agencies rely on is standby or on-call status for assigning cases during periods of lighter workloads.

Across the country, homicide detectives can work a tremendous amount of overtime, with some detectives matching or exceeding their regular salary. In other agencies, officers accumulate overtime in the form of compensatory time off to be taken in the future. In some agencies, the traditional arrangement has been for detectives to work the number of hours necessary to solve the crime. In other departments, unit commanders must approve detectives' use of overtime. Some chiefs and commanders are hesitant to allow investigators to work extended hours because of the physical and mental toll of an investigation, which can lead to decreased productivity. Some departments report that defense attorneys are raising the issue of excessive hours and implying that it contributes to a decrease in investigator effectiveness.

Closely related to overtime is the question, "Who owns the case?" That is, does one detective (or two detectives working as partners) have primary responsibility for investigating the crime, or does responsibility rest with the entire homicide unit? If responsibility rests with one investigator who feels a strong commitment to solve the crime, then overtime can be more difficult to manage when that investigator wants to work extended shifts. A unit or team ownership model, in which investigative responsibilities are distributed among several investigators, can make managing overtime easier. In a team ownership model, a detective ending a shift can pass along information about the progress made to another detective starting the next shift. Instead of the first detective working excessive hours to continue the investigation, the detective starting a shift can take over from where the first detective left off in the investigation.

Departments must be aware of the competing concerns associated with overtime and must take the steps necessary to ensure it is used appropriately.

Take-Home Cars

Agencies provide take-home cars to investigators under a variety of arrangements. The primary advantage of providing officers with take-home cars is that it ensures a quicker response time to crime scenes.

Wellford (2000) found a positive correlation between the quick arrival of homicide detectives to a scene and the case being solved.[8] The primary disadvantages of take-home cars are that they require the department have a larger fleet of vehicles, accompanied by increased fuel and maintenance costs.

The Role of Crime Analysis

Some departments are examining how crime analysis can better assist in homicide investigations, both in serial murder and single murder investigations. Experience with problem-oriented policing and the SARA (Scanning, Analysis, Response and Assessment) model has enabled departments to identify distinct patterns in homicides that can lead to more effective investigations and strategies for preventing future homicides.[9] Crime analysts can conduct research and analysis and allow detectives more time for other functions, such as conducting interviews and following promising leads. In Austin, Texas, the police department's 12 crime analysts are divided among nine sectors and various investigative units. A supervisory analyst is assigned to the Robbery and Homicide Unit and assists investigators with a wide variety of tasks, including: creating wanted person flyers, performing database searches, developing timelines, analyzing telephone data, crime mapping, and performing link analyses. The products created assist during the investigation and can also be very powerful during trial presentations.

Some agencies have yet to adopt the use of crime analysis by homicide investigators. This is sometimes the result of staffing shortages in the crime analysis section, but in other agencies, detectives might be unsure of how to use crime analysts or may prefer to work the case alone, and thus are not always taking advantage of valuable resources.

---

8. Wellford, C. and J. Cronin. *Homicides: What Police Can Do to Improve Clearance Rates.* Washington, D.C.: National Institute of Justice, April 2–7, 2000.
9. Schmerler, Karen, et al., *Problem-Solving Tips: A Guide to Reducing Crime and Disorder Through Problem-Solving Partnerships.* Washington, D.C.: U.S. Department of Justice, Office of Community Oriented Policing Services, 2006.

CONSIDERATIONS

Based on the topics covered in this chapter, here is a checklist of questions a chief or homicide unit commander should consider:

- How does my community define effectiveness (clearance rates, number of annual homicides, conviction rates)?
- Do we need to modify the homicide unit's responsibilities to include other types of crime?
- Does our rotation policy enable detectives to function effectively?
- Are our detectives receiving the training they need to be effective?
- Does our selection process ensure that we choose successful detectives?
- What schedule should we use to increase investigator effectiveness?
- What can we do to enable investigators to arrive at homicide crime scenes as quickly as possible (e.g., take-home cars)?
- Do our overtime and standby pay policies facilitate effective case management?
- How can we take full advantage of the expertise of our crime analysts?
- Should we engage in various levels of case review?
- How do we ensure increased witness cooperation and strengthened community relationships?
- What other resources exist to assist my homicide unit?

4

Eyewitness Identification

EYEWITNESS IDENTIFICATION AND TESTIMONY ARE FUNDAmental to the United States criminal justice system. Eyewitnesses are crucial to solving crimes, and sometimes eyewitness identification is the only evidence available to police when charging someone with a crime; however, eyewitness testimony is not infallible. Memories can be faulty or incomplete and eyewitnesses can be uncertain or confused. In addition, some lineup procedures can actually make it more difficult for eyewitnesses to identify the culprit or reject an innocent person.

For almost 100 years, psychologists have studied human memory and its influence on eyewitness identification. Based on laboratory experiments and field studies, some psychologists have published recommendations aimed at making eyewitness identification procedures more reliable. And recent advancements in DNA have contributed to the exoneration of convicted persons, many of whom were convicted based on eyewitness identifications. In response to these developments, in 1999 the National Institute of Justice (NIJ) published a research report, *Eyewitness Evidence: A Guide for Law Enforcement*, which included specific guidelines for conducting lineups and photo arrays. That publication included discussion of research and practical perspectives on eyewitness identification, and provided recommendations to promote the accuracy and reliability of eyewitness evidence.[1]

---

1. *Eyewitness Evidence: A Guide for Law Enforcement*. Washington, D.C.: National Institute of Justice, 1999.

Relying on these guidelines, some law enforcement agencies have modified their lineup and photo array practices. Some of the modifications were made voluntarily, but in some jurisdictions state legislatures or court decrees mandated the changes. Other states continue to study the issue, and some are leaning toward modifying their procedures. The goal has always been to protect the innocent and identify the guilty.

Yet not everyone is convinced that these new procedures are more effective than those that have been used for many years. A recent study by the State of Illinois actually found sequential lineups *less* effective than methods traditionally used by law enforcement agencies (e.g., simultaneous lineups).[2] The Illinois study has caused some states to reconsider the changes they have mandated, and has created uncertainty in the minds of police agency administrators about which procedures they should adopt.

This chapter provides guidance to agencies struggling to make sense of the different, and sometimes conflicting, advice circulating in criminal justice circles. It provides background on the research on human memory, presents results from recent field experiments, discusses the benefits and disadvantages of different procedures, and provides a series of questions agencies should consider when deciding whether to modify their eyewitness identification policies and procedures.

DEFINITIONS

It is important to have a common understanding of the terms used by law enforcement officers and psychologists who study eyewitness testimony. For instance, the first two terms—culprit and suspect—while seemingly similar, are very different.

- **Culprit(s)**—The person(s) who actually committed the crime.

- **Suspect(s)**—The person(s) law enforcement officers believe to be the culprit.

- **Fillers**—People known not to be suspects (or culprits) who populate the lineup.

---

[2]. Mecklenburg, Sheri H. *Report to the Legislature of the State of Illinois: The Illinois Pilot Program on Sequential Double-Blind Identification Procedures.* 2006.

- **Show-ups**—A procedure in which a suspect is detained, usually in a public place, to allow an eyewitness to determine if the suspect is the culprit.

- **Lineup**—A procedure in which a criminal suspect is placed among fillers to allow an eyewitness the opportunity to identify the suspect as the culprit.

- **Photo arrays**—A procedure in which a photograph of the suspect, either paper or on a computer screen, is placed among photographs of fillers to allow an eyewitness the opportunity to identify the suspect as the culprit.

- **Simultaneous**—A lineup or photo array procedure in which the eyewitness views all lineup members or photographs at the same time.

- **Sequential**—A lineup or photo array procedure in which the eyewitness views lineup members or photographs one at a time, and is required to make a decision before viewing the next lineup member.

- **Double blind**—A procedure used in lineups or photo arrays in which the law enforcement official administering the lineup or photo array has not been told by his colleagues in the police department which person is a suspect. Thus, the term double-blind means that neither the administrator nor the eyewitness is told which person in the lineup or photo array is the suspect.

THE RESEARCH

Human memory has long been a topic of research in the field of psychology, and for the past century it has been the subject of inquiry and experimentation. Using filmed events and staged crimes, psychologists have found that eyewitnesses frequently make mistakes, even when they are confident in their ability to recall events and identify culprits. Thinking of the human eye as a camera and the mind as a videotape is not a good analogy. Rather, people interpret what they see in many different ways, and their memories can be altered by external influences and can fade over time.

For years, psychologists tried to persuade officials in the criminal justice system, especially the courts, of the problems that faulty human memory can have in identifying culprits correctly, but they made little progress.[3] The court system's resistance to change is attributable to several factors, including the incremental nature of research, the conservative nature of the judiciary, and the topic of memory itself. Human memory and recall are fundamental parts of being human, and people have strong feelings about them. While most people agree that we might forget certain things, most people do not believe that we remember things incorrectly. But the research into human memory demonstrates that people do, in fact, remember things incorrectly, and that our memories change. These variations in memory apply to everyday events as well as traumatic events, such as witnessing a crime.

Two things changed how the criminal justice system viewed this research. One was the significant number of death-row exonerations that have occurred since 1989 as a result of advances in DNA. In many of those exonerations, the primary evidence in the original conviction was eyewitness testimony. Some estimate that as many as 75 percent of the original convictions were the result of mistaken eyewitness identification.[4]

The other development that changed how the criminal justice system viewed psychological research into eyewitness identification occurred earlier, in 1978, when Gary Wells made a breakthrough distinction between system variables (e.g., police procedures) and estimator variables (e.g., lighting of the crime scene).[5] System variables are those things that can be controlled by the criminal justice system, and estimator variables are those things that are beyond the control of the system. Research up to this time had focused on both variables but had not made a distinction between them. This distinction began to break down an incredibly complex issue into more understandable parts. It enabled behavioral scientists and criminal justice practitioners to understand the implications of the research findings on using eyewitness identification in investigations and trials.

---

3. Doyle, James M. *True Witness: Cops, Courts, Science and the Battle against Misidentification.* New York: Palgrave Macmillan, 2005.
4. *Understand the Causes: Eyewitness Misidentification.* The Innocence Project. http://www.innocenceproject.org
5. Wells, Gary L. "Applied Eyewitness Testimony Research: System Variables and Estimator Variables." *Journal of Applied Social Psychology* 36 (1978): 1546–57.

Estimator Variables

Estimator variables are factors relating to human memory and are beyond the control or influence of the criminal justice system. These include the setting or lighting of the crime scene and whether the victim and offender are of the same or different races. Wells grouped estimator variables into four main categories:

1. Characteristics of the witness, including things such as age, race, intelligence, and personality.
2. Characteristics of the event, including the distinctiveness of the culprit, the amount of time the culprit was in view, the lighting, and the presence or absence of a weapon.
3. Characteristics of the testimony, including witness accuracy, speed, and certainty in identifying the culprit in a lineup.
4. The ability of others to differentiate between accurate and inaccurate testimony, including jurors' judgments about eyewitness identification accuracy.

Again, these variables are beyond the control of the criminal justice system. They cannot be modified or influenced. For this reason, this chapter will only identify them and will focus more on system variables.

System Variables

System variables affect the accuracy of eyewitness identifications and can be controlled by criminal justice agencies. System variables primarily refer to the procedures police investigators use in obtaining eyewitness identifications, and fall into four categories:

1. Instructions.
2. Lineup content.
3. Lineup presentation method.
4. Behavioral influence of the lineup administrator.

Before discussing these variables in detail, however, it is important to discuss how lineups are affected by the presence or absence of the actual culprit. Not all lineups contain the culprit. One way this can occur is when law enforcement officials mistakenly believe a suspect is the culprit. The suspect is actually innocent, resulting in a culprit-absent lineup. Or in some cases, investigators may use a lineup to eliminate one or more suspects, none of whom is the actual culprit. Again, this could create a culprit-absent lineup. Irrespective of the reasons for the culprit-absent lineup, witnesses will approach the lineup as if the culprit is present.

Research has demonstrated that witnesses tend to select a person from the lineup who most resembles their *memory* of the culprit at the time of the crime.[6] Researchers refer to this as the relative-judgment decision process, which can create a situation where a witness identifies a person from the lineup who is not the actual culprit, even though the witness believes his or her selection is correct. This also explains why eyewitnesses sometimes mistakenly pick someone out of a lineup even though the culprit is not present. The implications of this process will be discussed below.

Instructions

The first important system variable in eyewitness identifications is the pre-lineup instructions given to witnesses. Research has demonstrated that advising the eyewitness that the culprit "might or might not be present" reduced mistaken identifications in culprit-absent lineups, without compromising the ability of witnesses to select the culprit when he or she was present.[7]

Lineup Content

This variable concerns the makeup of the lineup, that is, the individuals who comprise the lineup. Seemingly a simple concept, the relationship among the persons in the lineup is rather complex. Research into these relationships has produced findings that, while intriguing, may have little

---

[6]. Wells, Gary L. "The Psychology of Lineup Identifications." *The Journal of Applied Social Psychology* 14 (1984): 89–103.
[7]. Steblay, Nancy M. "Social Influence in Eyewitness Recall: A Meta-analytic Review of Lineup Instruction Effects." *Law and Human Behavior* 21 (1997): 283–98.

practical application outside the research laboratory. The most relevant research, however, indicates that lineup fillers should reflect the eyewitness's description of the *culprit*. If the witness's description of the culprit is limited or sparse, or when the description of the culprit differs significantly from the appearance of the suspect, research indicates that the fillers should resemble the *suspect*.

Lineup Presentation Method

Research has examined the way in which lineups can be constructed, specifically the order in which eyewitnesses view participants. The research indicates that the sequential lineup may be more effective than the traditional simultaneous lineup. Sequential lineups are thought to reduce the effect of the relative judgment decision, because eyewitnesses must compare each member of the lineup (individually) to their memory of the culprit and not to other lineup members. The findings have been mixed. Several studies have shown that sequential lineups reduce the chances of mistaken identification in *culprit-absent* lineups;[8] however, the sequential method also reduces accurate identifications in *culprit-present* lineups.

Behavioral Influence of the Lineup Administrator

The final variable over which the criminal justice system has control is the person who administers the lineup. The most common approach in traditional lineups is for the case investigator to administer the lineup. This investigator, of course, knows which lineup member is the suspect and which ones are the fillers. Research in laboratory settings shows that when an administrator knows the true identity of the lineup members, he or she *can* influence, sometimes unwittingly, the eyewitness selection.[9] The same research shows that use of a "blind administrator"—one who

---

8. Steblay, Nancy M., Jennifer Dysart, Solomon Fulero, and R.C.L. Lindsay. "Eyewitness Accuracy Rates in Sequential and Simultaneous Lineup Presentations: A Meta-Analytic Comparison." *Law and Human Behavior* 25 (2001): 459–74.

9. Phillips, M.R., B.D. McAuliff, M.B. Kovera, and B. Cutler. "Double-Blind Photoarray Administration as a Safeguard Against Investigator Bias." *Journal of Applied Psychology*, 84 (1999): 940–51; Wells, G.L. and A.L. Bradfield. "Good, You Identified the Suspect: Feedback to Eyewitnesses Distorts Their Reports of the Witnessing Experience." *Journal of Applied Psychology*, 83 (1998): 360–76; Wells, G.L. and A.L. Bradfield. "Distortions in Eyewitness' Recollections: Can the Post-identification Feedback Effect Be Moderated?" *Psychological Science*, 10 (1999): 138–44.

cannot differentiate between the suspect and the fillers—reduces the opportunities to influence the eyewitness during and after the lineup.

Criminal Justice Initiatives to Improve Eyewitness Identification

Outside of academia, several initiatives have attempted to build on or apply the conclusions of research psychologists. Most notably, the NIJ in 1999 published a research report, *Eyewitness Evidence: A Guide for Law Enforcement*. The guide was the result of several years of working group meetings that included representatives from law enforcement, prosecution, criminal defense, and the judiciary. It includes guidelines on working with eyewitnesses from the point of the initial call for service to lineups. Drawing on research findings and practical experience, the guide provides specific instructions for conducting simultaneous and sequential lineups and photo arrays. While the guide includes procedures for sequential methods, it stopped short of endorsing sequential methods as more effective than simultaneous methods. Still, this was the first criminal justice publication to recognize the benefits of sequential identification procedures.

This document, and its companion piece on training officers to use the guidelines, published in 2003, coupled with post-conviction exonerations, prompted some jurisdictions to review their eyewitness identification procedures.

CURRENT LAW ENFORCEMENT PRACTICES AND POLICIES

A number of law enforcement agencies across the country have modified their policies on eyewitness identification as a result of the research and NIJ guidance. Some of the changes have been voluntary, but others were mandated by legislation, court decision or by the state attorney general. In most of the situations, however, the change in policy was in direct response to specific exonerations of convicted offenders within a state. Not every agency implemented the same changes. Many chose some combination of policies that drew on the academic research while also considering the practical implications of the policy changes on investigations. Some of the procedural changes have been subjected to research into their effectiveness, while in other situations no evaluation has occurred.

This section provides an overview of some of the changes and field experiments in eyewitness identification policy and procedure. No attempt is made to evaluate or critique the actions of the agencies or the methods and results of the researchers. Scientific critiques of the research are a necessary part of eventually reaching conclusions about the most effective policies to pursue. At times, however, the critiques can take on a life of their own, making it difficult to understand the implications of the research. Two recent journal articles illustrate the different, and sometimes competing, positions people have about this research and its implications. One article, written by a panel of social scientists, contends that the recent Illinois field study has fundamental methodological flaws that limit its contributions to eyewitness identification knowledge.[10] The other article, written by prosecutors, including the author of the Illinois study, argues that the Illinois study makes a significant contribution to the study of eyewitness identification and lays the groundwork for additional field studies.[11] The articles raise important points for police administrators and researchers to consider as we move from the laboratory to the station house.

It is safe to say that none of the field experiments replicate completely the conditions or protocols used in laboratories. This is to be expected because conditions in the laboratory are completely designed and controlled by researchers, whereas field experiments occur in real-life settings that are largely beyond the control of researchers and police administrators. In fact, in all of these field studies, researchers had to modify the research design to accommodate the challenges associated with homicide investigations. Usually, they explain these modifications and how they may have affected the study results. This section provides an overview of these studies and assesses how they can help administrators understand the complexities of eyewitness identification.

---

[10]. Schacter, Daniel L., et al. "Policy Forum: Studying Eyewitness Investigations in the Field." *Law and Human Behavior*, July 2007.

[11]. Mecklenburg, Sheri H., et al. "The Illinois Field Study: A Significant Contribution to Understanding Real World Eyewitness Identification Issues." *Law and Human Behavior*, August 2007.

New Jersey

On April 18, 2001, New Jersey became the first state in the nation to officially adopt the NIJ recommendations. As a result of DNA-based exonerations in New Jersey, and drawing on the NIJ recommendations, the New Jersey Attorney General issued *Guidelines for Preparing and Conducting Photo and Live Lineup Identification Procedures* (see Appendix C). The guidelines advised agencies "to utilize, whenever practical, someone other than the primary investigator assigned to the case to conduct both photo and live lineup identifications." In addition, the guidelines recommended that "when possible, sequential lineups should be utilized for both photo and live lineup identifications."

To assist with implementing the guidelines, the State Division of Criminal Justice worked with state and local agencies to train investigators. A 2003 survey found that law enforcement agencies of every size throughout the state have used the sequential identification method, with 84 percent of the agencies estimating that they use the sequential identifications "in every case." Fewer agencies, however, report using the blind administrator, with only 62 percent reporting that they used one "in every case." Beyond collecting numbers about the estimated use of the two procedures, New Jersey has not published any evaluations of the program's implementation or effectiveness.[12]

Hennepin County

In the fall of 2003, the Hennepin County (Minnesota) District Attorney chose to study eyewitness identification procedures when she heard about new research on this topic and potential reforms. The county implemented a pilot program in four city police departments ranging from Minneapolis (population 380,000) to New Hope (population 21,000). The pilot project focused on felony cases in the four departments, and required that all lineups be administered as sequential double-blind. This requirement even applied to cases in which the crime victim knew the perpetrator. Because the study required all lineups to be administered double-blind and sequentially, the researchers did not

---

12. Mecklenburg, Sheri H. *Report to the Legislature of the State of Illinois: The Illinois Pilot Program on Sequential Double-Blind Identification Procedures.* 2006.

include comparison groups using different methods. Ultimately, the project involved 280 lineups over a 12-month period ending in November 2004.

The Hennepin County pilot project sought to answer two questions: 1. whether the number and quality of identifications would change with the blind sequential lineup procedure, and 2. whether police departments could implement the procedures smoothly and effectively. The departments were asked to adhere to the following procedures:[13]

- **Effective lineup construction:** Lineups had to include six members—one suspect and five fillers, with fillers chosen to match the witness's description of the perpetrator.

- **Cautionary (unbiased) instruction:** The witness had to be instructed that the perpetrator might or might not be in the lineup.

- **Confidence statement:** A statement of witness confidence, in the witness's own words, had to be recorded at the time of the identification and before any feedback. The procedure allowed for but did not demand a witness comment for each photo.

- **Blind administration:** The lineup administrator could not know who the suspect was, and the witness was told that the administrator did not know which lineup member was the suspect.

- **Sequential presentation:** Lineup photos were presented one at a time, with the witness making a decision about each photo before the next was presented. The witness was not allowed to compare photos side by side at any time. The full sequence was completed even if an early identification was made, and the witness was informed that this completion is required by the procedure.

To answer the first question about whether the number and quality of identifications would change with the blind sequential lineup procedure, the project relied on 280 double-blind sequential lineups from 117 cases, which included 206 eyewitnesses. The results of the Hennepin

---

13. Klobuchar, Amy, Nancy M. Steblay, and Hilary Caliguiri. "Improving Eyewitness Identifications: Hennepin County's Blind Sequential Lineup Pilot Project." *Cardozo Public Law, Policy and Ethics Journal,* April 2006.

County study produced suspect identification rates comparable to results from similar laboratory and field tests, including fewer witnesses identifying fillers as the culprit. Repeated viewings of the photographs, however, increased the chances of witnesses selecting a filler—an innocent person. Repeated viewings of a sequential lineup may have the same effects as a simultaneous lineup, introducing the relative judgment decision process.

The study did not indicate that sequential double-blind lineups inhibited "jump-out" identifications, in which the witness has an immediate and emotional response. And, consistent with expectations, suspect identification rates were significantly lower for strangers than for familiar perpetrators.

The answer to the second question, whether police departments could implement the procedures smoothly and effectively, is "yes," despite some initial misgivings about the new protocols. The pilot project indicated that the double-blind sequential protocol is workable for police in both large and small departments without undercutting the ability to solve cases. (Although the agencies had some early problems with the protocol, these were resolved within a few months.) The study authors concluded that blind-sequential lineups work well, resulting in acceptable suspect identification rates and decreased filler identification rates. (In addition, anecdotal evidence suggests that eyewitnesses are providing stronger evidence in the courtroom.[14])

Illinois

In 2003, the Illinois legislature passed a law requiring the state police to conduct a 1-year pilot study to assess the effectiveness of the sequential double-blind procedure in the field. The primary research question was whether such procedures are more effective than simultaneous procedures, with the measure of effectiveness being a lower number of known false identifications. Three Illinois police departments participated in the study: Chicago (population 2,896,000), Joliet (population 106,000), and Evanston (population 74,000).

---

14. Steblay, Nancy. "Observations on the Illinois Lineup Data." Minneapolis: Augsberg College, 2006.

The research design for this project included each department determining its own protocol for randomly selecting which cases would use the sequential double-blind procedure and which cases would use the simultaneous procedure. In all cases, investigators informed witnesses that the offender might or might not be in the lineup. In the sequential procedure, witnesses had to provide a yes or no answer for each suspect presented to them and could view photographs only twice and in the same order. Data collection began in late 2004 and continued for 1 year, resulting in more than 700 simultaneous and sequential photo arrays and live lineups.

The project's final report showed that the double-blind, sequential identifications, when compared to simultaneous identifications, *produced a higher rate of filler identifications and lower rate of suspect identifications.*

In addition, the study uncovered problems with implementing the sequential presentation and blind administrator components. The sequential procedure created problems for live lineups, especially in cases with multiple offenders. The blind administrator component was especially troublesome, and caused some significant delays in conducting identifications or in conducting identifications outside of the stationhouse. Because of problems in always being able to find a blind administrator, this requirement was modified when there were multiple suspects.

Wisconsin

After examining wrongful convictions based on misidentification and social science research on eyewitness identification procedures, the Wisconsin Attorney General's Office in September 2005 issued the *Model Policy and Procedure for Eyewitness Identification*.[15] The model policy incorporates six major recommendations made by the scientific community:

1. Use nonsuspect fillers chosen to minimize any suggestiveness that might point toward the suspect.

2. Use a double-blind procedure, ensuring that the administrator is not in a position to unintentionally influence the witness's selection.

---

15. State of Wisconsin, Office of the Attorney General. *Model Policy and Procedure for Eyewitness Identification,* 2005.

3. Inform eyewitnesses that the real culprit may or may not be present and that the administrator does not know which person is the suspect.

4. Present the suspect and the fillers sequentially rather than simultaneously. Because eyewitnesses are unable to see the subjects all at once and are unable to know when they have seen the last subject, this procedure was believed to discourage relative judgment and encourage absolute judgments of each person presented.

5. Assess eyewitness confidence immediately after identification.

6. Do not use repeated photo arrays and lineups in which the same witness views the same suspect more than once.

This model policy was designed to ensure that the highest quality of evidence is obtained from eyewitnesses, while recognizing that there may be several ways to implement the principles of the policy, depending on the resources of individual law enforcement agencies. The new policies and procedures in Wisconsin have not yet been subjected to an evaluation.

North Carolina

On May 19, 2005, the Criminal Justice Standards Division of the North Carolina Department of Justice endorsed recommendations set forth in the North Carolina Actual Innocence Commission's report, *Recommendations for Eyewitness Identification*.[16] Although the following recommendations are not mandatory, they were incorporated into the Criminal Investigation lesson plan of the Basic Law Enforcement Training Course.

- Live lineups and photographic identifications should be presented sequentially rather than simultaneously.

- The individual conducting the photographic identification or live lineup should not know the identity of the actual suspect. Simultaneous

---

[16]. North Carolina Department of Justice, Criminal Justice Standards Division. *Recommendations for Eyewitness Identification*, May 19, 2005.

live lineups and photographic identifications may be used if a department does not have personnel available to conduct a double-blind procedure, but departments should be prepared to articulate in court why they used a simultaneous procedure.

- Witnesses should be told that the suspect may or may not be in the live lineup or photographic identification.

- A minimum of six photos should be used in photographic identification procedures.

- A minimum of six individuals should be used in live lineup procedures.

- Witnesses should not receive any feedback during or after the identification process.

- Witnesses should be asked to give feedback to the administrator in their own words regarding their level of confidence in their identification.

The largest local law enforcement agency in the state, the Charlotte-Mecklenburg Police Department, modified its eyewitness identification procedures to incorporate double-blind sequential lineups (see Appendix D). The department no longer routinely asks witnesses about their level of confidence, however, because prosecutors prefer to address this issue on a case-by-case basis. In July 2007, a bill was sent to the governor for signature that would require the use of blind administrators and sequential viewing of photographs or live persons.[17]

Other Agencies

A number of other agencies across the nation have modified their eyewitness identification policies. The Boston Police Department's modified policies include sequential lineups and use of the blind administrator procedure whenever possible. Another department in Massachusetts, the

---

17. The bill was signed on August 23, 2007: http://64.233.167.104/search?q=cache:
_ZYdtNDiBNgJ:web.austin.utexas.edu/law_library/innocence/subject.cfm%3Fsubject%
3D2+north+carolina+governor+double+blind+lineups&hl=en&ct=clnk&cd=8&gl=us and
http://www.ncga.state.nc.us/gascripts/BillLookUp/BillLookUp.pl?Session=2007&BillID=H1625

So, What Now? A Little Advice and Much Encouragement for Future Lineup Studies in the Field
by Nancy Steblay, Ph.D., Augsburg College

DNA exoneration cases have exposed eyewitness error as the predominant factor in false convictions. Almost a decade ago, this fact propelled joint action among law enforcement, legal professionals, and researchers, resulting in the 1999 publication of *Eyewitness Evidence: A Guide for Law Enforcement* by the National Institute of Justice.[18] The guide provided science-based recommendations for effective lineups and alerted law enforcement to three developing ideas for future refinement: double-blind lineup administration, sequential lineup presentation format, and the use of computers for lineup delivery.

Since then, researchers have produced a solid body of laboratory evidence that supports the use of double-blind sequential lineups as a means to secure better quality eyewitness identifications.[19] While the scientists anticipate that law enforcement will see gains in eyewitness accuracy similar to those found in the laboratory, law enforcement seeks evidence that the recommended changes actually aid eyewitness investigations. Also, as lineup reforms are implemented, it is likely that law enforcement departments will tinker with the new procedures, meld their past-preferred methods with the new ones, and perhaps generate speculation about how their revisions affect eyewitness accuracy. Questions are likely, including these:

1. How will we know if results from revised field lineups are really better? With a laboratory experiment, the scientist can definitively detect

---

18. Technical Working Group for Eyewitness Accuracy. *Eyewitness Evidence: A Guide for Law Enforcement, Research Report*, Washington, D.C.: U.S. Department of Justice, 1999.

19. Steblay, N., J. Dysart, S. Fulero, and R.C.L. Lindsay. "Eyewitness Accuracy Rates in Sequential and Simultaneous Lineup Presentations: A Meta-Analytic Comparison." *Law and Human Behavior*, 25 (2001): 459–473.

correct eyewitness decisions because the perpetrator's identity is known. In the field, however, the true status of the suspect is unknown. The worst-case scenario—when a witness's selection is incorrectly judged as accurate—is illustrated by many DNA exoneration cases.[20] Even the meaning of an eyewitness's failure to choose the suspect is not always clear; this may indicate that the witness has a poor memory *or* that the true culprit is not in the lineup. Field data alone tell us very little about witness reliability, but we *can* get to a reasonable answer from here.

2. Left with measures that offer no absolute standard of "goodness," what should we do?

Sound eyewitness evidence depends on the conditions under which the eyewitness makes the decision. Similarly, reliable study data are the result of sound scientific method and tested techniques of lineup construction and presentation.[21] One requisite safeguard for all lineups must be highlighted: the double-blind method.

Double-blind serves a dual role in lineup reforms. As a scientific tool, it provides the necessary method for objective comparisons of competing lineup strategies (e.g., to test sequential versus simultaneous formats). And in the real world of policing, the double-blind is an essential component for shielding the witness's lineup decision from the threat or even suspicion of unintentional administrator influence.[22]

---

20. *Understanding the Causes: Witness Misidentification*. The Innocence Project. http://www.innocence project.org

21. See, e.g., Wells, G.L., M. Small, S. Penrod, R.S. Malpass, S.M. Fulero, and C.A.E. Brimacombe. "Eyewitness Identification Procedures: Recommendations for Lineups and Photospreads." *Law and Human Behavior* 22 (1998): 603–647.

22. See, e.g., Haw, R. and R.P. Fisher. "Effects of Administrator-Witness Contact on Eyewitness Identification Accuracy." *Journal of Applied Psychology* 89 (2004): 1106–1112; McQuiston-Surrett, D., R.S. Malpass, and C.G. Tredoux. "Sequential vs. Simultaneous Lineups: A Review of Methods, Data, and Theory." *Psychology, Public Policy, and Law* 122 (2004): 147–169; Phillips, M.R., B.D. McAuliff, M.B. Kovera, and B.L. Cutler. "Double-Blind Photoarray Administration as a Safeguard against Investigator Bias." *Journal of Applied Psychology* 84 (1999): 940–951; Rosenthal, R. and D.B. Rubin. (1978). "Interpersonal Expectancy Effects: The First 345 Studies." *Behavioral and Brain Sciences* 3 (1978): 377–386.

3. How can future collaboration between field and laboratory studies promote effective lineup procedures?

Recent field studies have underscored the need for scientists and law enforcement to work together to meet the requirements of rigorous scientific testing while also producing practical lessons for the street. Police investigators can provide insight about operational challenges and develop creative remedies. For example, when a blind administrator is not available, the envelope technique or laptop lineup delivery can be used. And more broadly, police and prosecutors can help scientists frame future research questions.[23]

Input from scientists can be particularly helpful when a jurisdiction amends its guidelines. Experiments can determine whether changes in procedure enhance or detract from the accuracy of eyewitness decisions. Some jurisdictions, for example, prefer that an eyewitness be allowed multiple viewings of the sequential lineup. Hennepin County (Minnesota) allowed multiple viewings and collected data from both field and lab. The findings converged: Field data showed increasing filler selections (known errors) with lineup laps; lab data echoed this pattern, establishing that misidentifications increased by 26 percent following repeated viewing of the lineup.[24]

Finally, any hope of producing useful findings will fade quickly if researchers, police, prosecutors, and interested observers do not have a specific and detailed lineup protocol or do not adhere to the one they have. Investigators have long-established habits for conducting lineups that do not always follow written departmental guidelines. It is important for departments to determine whether these habits are intentionally or inadvertently transferred to the new lineup routine. An effective scripting for new lineup standards must edit old practice and

---

23. Klobuchar, A., N.K.M. Steblay, and H.L. Caligiuri. "Improving Eyewitness Identifications: Hennepin County's Blind Sequential Lineup Pilot Project," *Cardozo Public Law, Policy, and Ethics Journal* 2 (2006): 381–414.

24. Steblay, N. *Double-Blind Sequential Police Lineup Procedures: Toward an Integrated Laboratory & Field Practice Perspective. Final Report:* Grant # 2004-IJ-CX-0044, National Institute of Justice, U.S. Department of Justice, 2007.

combine it with the new to form a clear, coherent, and scientifically sound package. Research findings cannot be interpreted if the terms of a study are not defined clearly.

4. What are we likely to gain from future field studies?

Convinced by the scientific lab data and motivated by the desire for greater confidence in eyewitness evidence, a number of jurisdictions have implemented double-blind sequential procedures, often with reported success. While some jurisdictions have received substantial attention and publicity, others have initiated reforms under the radar, without much fanfare and encountering little difficulty.[25] Smooth translation of lineup reforms to the field has not been the case for all departments, however, and concerns have been voiced regarding implementation problems and outcome effectiveness.[26] In the short run, additional field studies will help to immediately address these specific concerns.

But there is also the larger and very important objective: That we secure more accurate memory evidence from eyewitnesses. Scientists and the legal system's practitioners must continue to work together to bring genuine improvements into practice. ■

---

25. *Ibid.*
26. Mecklenburg, S. *Report to the Legislature of the State of Illinois: The Illinois Pilot Program on Sequential Double-blind Identification Procedures.* 2006. www.chicagopolice.org/IL%20Pilot%20on%20Eyewitness%20ID.pdf.

Northampton Police Department, uses the double-blind sequential procedure. In Santa Clara County, California, the District Attorney's Office issued a protocol strongly recommending the use of double-blind sequential procedures. The Virginia State Crime Commission, a legislative advisory body, recommended double-blind sequential identification procedures, and new and veteran officers were slated to receive training in these procedures.

AGENCY CONSIDERATIONS FOR EYEWITNESS IDENTIFICATION

The intent of this chapter was to provide an overview of the complex issue of eyewitness identification. The topic of human memory and recall, by itself, is exceedingly complex, and many questions about how humans store and recall memories remain unanswered. Psychological research studies, conducted under carefully designed and controlled protocols, have demonstrated that eyewitness identification is more effective under specific conditions. The challenge is to determine how to replicate those conditions when moving from the laboratory to the station house.

A number of agencies have attempted to do just that. Some have implemented double-blind sequential procedures, while others have chosen to experiment with the procedures before making any permanent changes. The agencies that have implemented changes indicate that the revised procedures are feasible. Modifying procedures is not without challenges, but the obstacles have been overcome by agencies large and small. Probably one of the biggest challenges is the use of a blind administrator to run the lineups. The first hurdle to overcome is the reluctance of investigators to allow someone else to run the lineup during a crucial part of the investigation. The notion of a blind administrator contains an implicit accusation that police officers harbor bias, lack integrity, or simply cannot be trusted. A second concern is whether a department has the personnel resources to have a blind administrator available around the clock and in different locations within a jurisdiction. That was a serious problem in the Illinois field study.

Several agencies have conducted field tests to evaluate different lineup procedures. These field tests are exceedingly complicated. Conducting psychological research in a laboratory setting is arduous; doing it in a police agency under real-life conditions adds several layers of complexity. Duplicating the protocols used in the laboratory is almost impossible; consequently, the study results do not always have the validity and reliability that researchers prefer. In examining the results of these field tests it is important to realize that each test is unique. Tests ask different research questions and are conducted in different settings, so naturally they will produce different results. And while researchers will critique the studies using one set of criteria, police administrators will want to rely on another set of criteria to determine if their agency should adopt new eyewitness identification procedures. The bottom line is that the research in the laboratory and the station house must continue, so that we can more fully understand eyewitness identification and its role in criminal investigations.

Despite the complexity of these issues, consensus is beginning to emerge among researchers and police administrators in several areas. Of course, not every practitioner or researcher unanimously agrees with each point. Based on research and practice, law enforcement agencies should examine their current policies and compare them to the following procedures to determine if they are appropriate for their agencies:

- **Instructions**—All eyewitnesses should be told that the culprit may or may not be present in the lineup.

- **Double blind**—Lineups should be administered by law enforcement personnel who do not know the identity of the culprit. Although implementing double-blind lineups may create operational challenges, many departments have overcome those challenges.

- **One suspect per lineup**—A lineup should include only one suspect.

- **Number of lineup members**—At least six photographs should be used in any photo array, and six persons in any live lineup.

- **Sequential**—To the extent possible, photographs and live lineup members should be presented sequentially to eyewitnesses.

- **Number of viewings**—Eyewitnesses should be limited to no more than two cycles, or laps, when viewing photographs; and the photographs should be presented in the same order. The lineup administrator should record the results of each lap.

Making Improvements to Eyewitness Identification Now

by Sheri H. Mecklenburg, former General Counsel to the Superintendent of the Chicago Police Department, and Coordinator of the Illinois Pilot Program on Eyewitness Identification

In 2006, Illinois released its findings on the first field study of sequential, double-blind lineups.[27] The study did not support the claims that the sequential, double-blind procedure was superior to the traditional lineup procedure.[28] Nor did the study prove that the sequential, double-blind method was inferior to the traditional lineup procedure. Nevertheless, the Illinois study should not be considered conclusive because it is only one study and, further, the data require careful analysis of issues inherent in any field data, as well as comparison with other reliable field data. The Illinois study proved that there is still much work to be done before the science underlying sequential, double-blind lineups meets the standard of proof that we should demand of any science in this post-DNA world.[29] The resulting uniform call for additional field studies recognizes the need for more work in this area.

As we struggle with the lessons learned from DNA exonerations and attempt to ensure against future injustices, it is regrettable that so much of the discussion on eyewitness identification has focused on whether the lineup is presented sequentially or simultaneously,

---

[27]. Mecklenburg, S. *Report to the Legislature of the State of Illinois: The Illinois Pilot Program on Sequential Double-blind Identification Procedures.* 2006. www.chicagopolice.org/IL%20Pilot%20on%20Eyewitness%20ID.pdf.

[28]. The data showed a 9.2 percent rate of filler identifications in sequential, double-blind lineups, compared to a 2.8 percent rate of filler identifications in the traditional lineups. *Id.*

[29]. Haddad, James P. et al. *Criminal Procedure Cases and Comments, Sixth Edition* (7th Edition forthcoming); Inbau, Fred E. *Criminal Law and Its Administration, Sixth Edition,* Chapter 11 B.; See also "Best Police Lineup Format Not Yet ID'd," *Chicago Tribune,* July 30, 2007; "Questions Raised Over New Trend in Police Lineups," *The New York Times,* April 19, 2006.

double-blind or not, when this issue simply does not address the eyewitness identification issues raised by many of the DNA exonerations. Many of the DNA exonerations involving mistaken eyewitness identification revealed issues of poor training, poor supervision, poor police work, and, sometimes, misconduct, most of which began long before, and continued long after, the lineup occurred. The facts that led to many of the erroneous convictions would not prompt a police chief to ponder a policy of sequential, double-blind lineups. Rather, the facts would cause a police chief to examine standards, training, and supervision when dealing with eyewitnesses. This does not mean that the method of presenting the lineup should not be explored, but the focus on the sequential, double-blind lineup has come at the cost of diverting attention from real improvements in eyewitness identification.

Many police departments do not have comprehensive, written standards on how to conduct eyewitness identifications. Many police departments do not have uniform instructions to give to an eyewitness viewing a lineup. Even fewer require that written instructions be provided to eyewitnesses viewing a lineup, despite the fact that written instructions protect both the integrity of the identification and the officers against false claims of influence. Many lineup reports are incomplete and ambiguous, the fault of both the submitting investigator and the approving supervisors.

Many seasoned investigators have never had formal training on eyewitness identification. They have never had training on false identifications, have never heard about studies on eyewitness identification, and are unaware of many of the eyewitness issues raised by the DNA exonerations. Most investigators have learned about eyewitness identification from other officers in the station, repeating both the good and the bad practices of their predecessors, as well as their predecessors' predecessors. For those who do receive training, it is often limited to the basics of how to assemble a lineup. Legislatures across the country are being urged to adopt the sequential, double-blind method of lineups as a matter of law; but, unfortunately, they are not being urged to fund meaningful training on eyewitness identification for all local law enforcement.

The Illinois Pilot Program has prompted law enforcement officials and social scientists to call for more field studies on the sequential, double-blind method, before adopting the method as policy. But law enforcement should not stand by idly for years, waiting for adequate field studies. Law enforcement, both internally and through joint task forces, should be setting standards and developing meaningful training for eyewitness identification. Law enforcement is an entity committed only to identifying the actual offender, rather than to proving or disproving any scientific theory.[30] This unique role demands that law enforcement lead the way now in addressing the known issues underlying false eyewitness identifications. ■

---

[30]. See Zagel, J. "Getting to Truth Before It Falls Into the Hands of the Lawyers: Pursuing Accuracy in Criminal Cases." *Loyola Public Interest Law Reporter*, 11:2, p. 17 et. seq. (Summer 2006).

- **Witness statements**—Witnesses should not be coached in any manner, and any statements should be in the witnesses' own words.

- **Lineup reports**—Agencies should develop and use more complete lineup reports. Many agencies simply use "identification" or "no identification" in their reports. Agencies should require more specificity about the selection (e.g., suspect, filler, no choice, and all members excluded), as well as level of eyewitness confidence and speed with which the identification was made, if applicable.

- **Training**—Investigators need training in, and written instructions for, carrying out new procedures.

- **Computers**—Agencies should consider using computers to arrange photo arrays, if possible.

Agency Considerations

For those agencies contemplating changes in policies and procedures, some questions to ponder include the following:

- Should my agency implement sequential identification procedures?
- What does the jurisdiction's prosecutor think about the police procedures?
- Should my agency implement a double-blind procedure?
- What are the challenges to doing eyewitness identifications correctly?
- Should we implement new procedures in only a portion of the department to determine their effectiveness before going departmentwide?
- Can we link with university professors and researchers to help us design and evaluate any new procedures?
- When should we use photographs, and when should we use live lineups?
- How many photos or people should we use?
- How should we document witness recollections?

- What facilities and equipment do we need?
- What training do detectives need in any new procedures?
- Can we use multiple procedures in the agency?
- Can computer imaging or technology help?

CONCLUSION

The psychological research on human memory is compelling. The research on eyewitness identification is persuasive, but the methods and results are not always applicable when transferred from the laboratory to the station house. Although consensus exists in some areas, it does not exist in every area. The recent findings from the Illinois Pilot Study raise important questions about double-blind, sequential identifications. The Illinois study, along with all others, should be considered in light of all available evidence. Clearly, additional research is needed to help law enforcement agencies determine the most effective practices, and that research must be a collaborative effort between practitioners and researchers. In the meantime, agencies considering making changes to their eyewitness identification procedures should review the questions outlined above and, whenever possible, confer with agencies that have experience using various procedures.

5

Videotaped Interrogations

"Consider... the immeasurable value of giving the eventual jury the opportunity to hear, if not see, the defendant before he has thought to temper his attitude, clean up his language,... and otherwise soften his commonly offensive physical appearance, and you begin to appreciate the tremendous value of a taped interview."[1]

ANONYMOUS PROSECUTOR,
SAN DIEGO, CALIFORNIA

POLICE DEPARTMENTS OFTEN FACE INTERNAL CHALLENGES when instituting a significant change in the way they operate. Many departments that have adopted videotaped interrogations are, for the most part, satisfied with the results. Further, many would not be inclined to revert to traditional methods and stop videotaping interrogations, given the benefits derived from the practice. While not every investigator or manager is a proponent of videotaped interrogations, many seasoned investigators from departments across the country who have experience with videotaping interrogations prefer this method.

Videotaping interrogations has become more viable as a result of four influences: 1. prosecutors find the recordings incredibly powerful, and defense attorneys are less likely to question the practices of the police,

---

1. Sullivan, T. *Police Experiences with Recording Custodial Interrogations.* Northwestern University School of Law, Center on Wrongful Convictions. Special Report, 2004.

2. affordable technological advancements, 3. a realization that video monitoring is an accepted practice in many agencies, and 4. the desire in law enforcement to strengthen the evidence to convict offenders.

The prevalence of videotaping and digital technology in all of society has permeated law enforcement, as well. Many departments have shifted from VHS storage archives to completely digital recording and storage methods. The equipment is more affordable than it was in the past and more feasible for departments on a minimal budget. Further, video recording technology has had a recent surge in deployment for the detection and identification of criminal activity in many cities throughout the country. Many police cars today are outfitted with cameras to capture actions related to police stops, and as agencies have become comfortable with that type of recording, they have more easily accepted video recording of interviews and interrogations.

This chapter discusses current trends in videotape interrogations, including the benefits of recording and the challenges it presents, and identifies various factors law enforcement departments can consider regarding videotape protocols.

IN PRACTICE: THE VIDEOTAPE RECORDING OF INTERROGATIONS

What do we know about current videotaping practices?

Before the 1980s, most confessions were written or sometimes audiotaped. These methods, especially the written confessions, made it difficult for judges and juries to decide whether a statement was voluntary because of the inability to *see* how it was obtained. During the 1980s, some law enforcement agencies began videotaping interrogations so that trial participants could see exactly what occurred. In 1990 departments were surveyed about their videotape practices[2] and the study concluded that one-third of law enforcement agencies serving populations of more than 50,000 were videotaping some portion of interrogations.

---

2. Geller, W. *Videotaping Interrogations and Confessions.* Washington, D.C.: National Institute of Justice, Research in Brief. NCJ #139962, 1993; Geller, W. *Police Videotaping of Suspect Interrogations and Confessions: A Preliminary Examination of the Issues and Practices.* Washington, D.C.: Police Executive Research Forum, 1993.

Currently, some research indicates more than half of the state and local agencies nationwide videotape at least some interrogations.[3] Some federal agencies rely on videotaped interrogations, as well. Several departments are being mandated to videotape interrogations. Unlike lineup protocol discussions, videotaping mandates are not a result of academic research identifying empirical benefits to videotaping. On the contrary, a lack of quantitative research in this area makes it difficult to support or refute the outcomes associated with videotaping interrogations.

For example, Geller, in a study of attitudes and opinions about videotape interrogations, reported that departments claim videotaped interrogations led to more guilty pleas, longer sentences, and more convictions.[4] Another effort to study videotaping was conducted in conjunction with the Center on Wrongful Convictions.[5] The study included surveys and interviews with more than 400 departments about videotaping legislation and protocols. This descriptive study helps explain the prevalence of videotaping and officer attitudes toward it, but does not evaluate whether recording produces higher conviction rates.

Why are departments videotaping?

Several states, including California, Illinois, Maine, and New Mexico, have been mandated by state or local legislation to videotape interrogations. In 2005, the District of Columbia was also mandated to do so. Alaska, Massachusetts, Minnesota, New Hampshire, New Jersey, and Wisconsin have been mandated to videotape by State Supreme Court rulings. During the 2005–2006 legislative session, 44 bills were introduced in the states relating to electronic recording of interrogations. The strong interest among state legislators in electronic recording of interrogations can be generally attributed to a handful of committed groups working to uncover wrongful criminal convictions and bring them to the forefront of legislative agendas. There doesn't appear to be any one event

---

[3]. Moorman, J. "Confessions of a Dangerous Kind." *Perspectives*. Athens, Ohio: Ohio University, 2005.
[4]. Geller, W. *Videotaping Interrogations and Confessions*. Washington, D.C.: National Institute of Justice, Research in Brief. NCJ #139962, 1993.
[5]. Sullivan, T. *Police Experiences with Recording Custodial Interrogations*. Northwestern University School of Law, Center on Wrongful Convictions. Special Report, 2004.

or case that has ignited the attention, but rather a national call to address the interrogation process which often leads to evidence for or against a conviction.[6]

The majority of mandates have resulted from a wrongful conviction case or string of cases or the desire to follow the lead of other jurisdictions that have adopted videotaping and cite promising results, or both. Table 2 highlights a number of legislative actions, to date, that involve recording of interrogations. Note that most require only "electronic recording," not necessarily video recording. Table 3 identifies case law,

Table 2. **Recent State Laws on Videotaped Interrogation**[7]

State	Legislation — Passed	Year
District of Columbia	*Electronic Recording Procedures Act* — Requires electronic recording of custodial interrogation relating to crimes of violence	2004
Illinois	*Recorded Statements Act & Amendment to Require Recorded Interrogations in DUI Related Deaths* — Requires electronic recording of custodial interrogations of juveniles, homicide suspects, and persons suspected of DUI-related deaths	2005
Maine	*An Act to Require the Videotaping of Police Interrogations* — Requires videotaping of all custodial "examinations" concerning the commission of a crime	2004
New Mexico	*An Act Relating to Law Enforcement* — Requires electronic recording of custodial interrogations in felony cases	2005
Texas	*Texas Code of Criminal Procedure 38.22* — Requires electronic recording of all custodial statements	2001
Wisconsin	*AB 648* — Requires electronic recording of custodial interrogations of adults in felony cases and juveniles	2005

---

6. Personal Communication with Scott Ehlers, Director of State Legislative Affairs, National Association of Criminal Defense Lawyers, January 22, 2007.

7. National Association of Criminal Defense Lawyers. www.nacdl.org

briefs, and motions that have affected law enforcement practices on videotape interrogations.

Other departments have voluntarily opted to videotape interrogations because of the perceived benefit. For example, the Detroit Police Department recently began videotaping all interrogations where the suspect is facing the possibility of a life sentence. This decision was the result

Table 3. **Case Law, Briefs and Motions**[8]

State	Case Law, Briefs, and Motions	Year
Alaska	*Stephan v. State* — The Alaska Supreme Court held that an unexcused failure to record custodial interrogations violated the suspect's right to due process under the state constitution. Custodial interviews must be electronically recorded.	1985
Massachusetts	*Commonwealth v. DiGiambiattista* — The Massachusetts Supreme Judicial Court held that when an interrogation is not at least audiotaped, a jury instruction may be requested.	2004
Minnesota	*State v. Scales* — The Minnesota Supreme Court held that custodial interrogations must be recorded.	1994
New Hampshire	*State v. Barnett* — The New Hampshire Supreme Court held that if a recorded final statement is offered into evidence, the recording is admissible only if the entire post-Miranda interrogation is recorded.	2001
New Jersey	*Rule 3:17: Electronic Recordation* — Court rule requiring recordings of custodial interrogations, and jury instructions to be given in the absence of a recorded statement.	2005
Wisconsin	*State v. Jerrell* — The Wisconsin Supreme Court required that all custodial interrogations of juveniles be electronically recorded.	2005

---

8. National Association of Criminal Defense Lawyers. www.nacdl.org

of the wrongful conviction of Eddie Joe Lloyd, who spent 17 years in prison for the rape and murder of Michelle Jackson, a 16-year-old. Lloyd had a psychiatric history and confessed to the homicide during his interrogation. He was later exonerated of the crime by DNA analysis. The Lloyd family settlement with the city, county and state is reportedly more than $4 million.[9]

The Denver Police Department began videotaping interviews in 1983 to foster a greater level of transparency in its investigative interviewing methods in officer-involved shooting cases. At that time, the department had only one videotape interview room. Over time, because of the positive experiences the department had with the practice, other units, including homicide, gained interest in using the videotaping rooms for their investigations. The number of videotape interview rooms eventually increased to 25 throughout the city. The number of videotaped interviews has increased tenfold since 1983 (see Figure 4). Denver now has the ability to videotape suspect, victim, and witness interviews in all crime types.

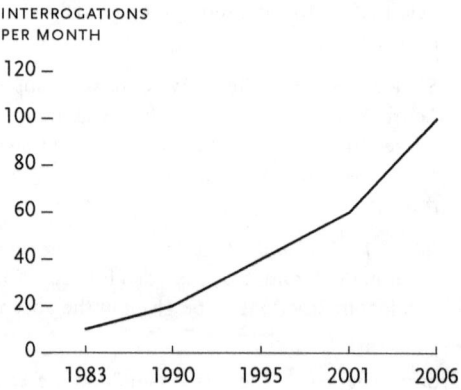

Figure 4. **Number of Denver Police Department Videotaped Interviews from 1983 to 2006**[10]

---

9. "Wrongful Conviction Prompts Detroit Police to Videotape Certain Interrogations." *The New York Times*, April 11, 2006, A14.

10. Priest, Jonathyn W. (Lieutenant, Denver Police Department). Multiple personal interviews, June 2005.

VIDEOTAPED INTERROGATION PROCEDURES

What is being videotaped?

Departments videotape different segments of interrogations. Some videotape only the confession or final statement. Others videotape the interrogation but not the pre-interview. Others videotape the entire interrogation, from the reading of the Miranda rights to the end of the interview. The criteria regarding how much to videotape are established at the departmental level or through legislation. The decisions can be based on 1. identifying what is sufficient to succeed in court or is acceptable to the prosecutor's office, 2. a desire not to share too much of the department's investigative techniques with juries, and/or 3. consent requirements (dual-party consent states require the suspect to consent to the videotape proceedings).

Who is being videotaped?

Who is videotaped is another factor that varies by agency. The sensitive nature of some charges, coupled with the possibility of a life prison term or a death sentence, will often cause a department to videotape to provide transparency and a more detailed understanding to the jury of what transpired, and dispel the possibility that illegitimate tactics secured the confession or interrogation findings, which could contribute to a wrongful conviction. Some departments videotape only felony cases. Other departments, such as Detroit, base the decision on the sentence associated with the charge. If the suspect is facing a possibility of a life sentence, the department will videotape. Departments often videotape interviews or interrogations in cases involving sex crimes or child sex crimes. For example, the FBI's Phoenix Field Office videotapes all victim and witness statements in sexual assault cases involving children in Indian country. Some departments automatically videotape interrogations of juveniles and non-English-speaking suspects.

Some departments also videotape witness statements and are also more likely to videotape the entire interrogation of the suspect. These videotapes can be used in cases where the witness is unable to take the stand in court. Further, videotaped interviews and statements enable judges, defense attorneys, and juries to observe the behavior of the

The Miranda Warning–Videotaping Connection
by Lt. Jonathyn Priest, Denver Police Department

On June 13, 1966, the Supreme Court of the United States issued an opinion in *Miranda* v. *Arizona*. That decision resulted in what we in law enforcement call the Miranda advisement. At the time, police officers believed that the result of *Miranda* would be an end to obtaining confessions from suspects. But that did not happen; every day suspects continue to confess to crimes after being read their Miranda rights. When I became a police officer in 1980, I knew what Miranda was and that suspects always had to be read their rights. *Miranda* has never been a problem for me.

Many in law enforcement today view video interviewing the same way. These changes are seen as threats, and some may think, "We will no longer get what we did before this recording came in." I have experienced interviewing pre- and post-video and find that the video interview is, by far, more powerful. Law enforcement officials I have had the opportunity to meet agree: Once they begin to use this new video technology, they would never consider going backward. The officers of today see this video technology and never question what a suspect might do on camera. Law enforcement is an ever-changing profession that requires our ability to adapt and change to continue our pursuit of justice. ∎

witness and interactions between the witness and the detective, and to gain a more thorough understanding of the case than they would from a written statement.

BENEFITS OF VIDEOTAPING INTERROGATIONS

Departments that videotape interrogations identify a host of benefits in using this method. In addition, prosecutors and courts benefit from videotaped interrogations. The most often-cited strengths of videotaping interrogations are the following:

1. Provides transparency to the interview process. Viewers can observe the interaction between investigator(s) and suspects and/or witnesses.

2. Allows the detective greater focus on the suspect and/or witness.

3. Decreases cross-examination of detectives in court, and defense arguments that a suspect was coerced.

4. Allows for direct observation of suspect intent and statements.

5. Allows for lifetime review of the exact testimony for case review and interrogation training.

Transparency

Community policing has demonstrated the importance of promoting trust and stability in relationships between community members and law enforcement representatives. In recent years, many departments have become more forthright about their policies, procedures, and decisions, including the interview and interrogation process. By videotaping, these departments have enjoyed the benefit of showing the community how they conduct interrogations. Geller (1993)[11] found that videotaped interrogations also helped to encourage fair treatment of suspects and respect for their civil rights, and reduced stress on officers who, in the

---

11. Geller, W. *Videotaping Interrogations and Confessions.* Washington, D.C.: National Institute of Justice, Research in Brief. NCJ #139962, 1993; Geller, W. *Police Videotaping of Suspect Interrogations and Confessions: A Preliminary Examination of the Issues and Practices.* Washington, D.C.: Police Executive Research Forum, 1993.

past, might have had to defend their tactics and behaviors. This transparency has benefits for investigators and officers, who now have a measure of protection against allegations of coercion by those being interviewed. By demystifying the interview process, departments demonstrate that they have nothing to hide, which can foster greater community trust.

Focus

Videotaping has improved interview and interrogation procedures. When detectives spend too much energy on taking notes during an interview or interrogation, it can be distracting for the subject, and can impede the dialogue. When a recording device is used, detectives can better focus on observing and interacting with the suspect and/or witness. At the same time, subjects' anxiety may be lessened because they are not focused on, or concerned about, the detective's note-taking.

Courtroom Benefits

The general consensus among agencies is that videotaped interrogations help in courtroom proceedings. Lt. Jonathyn W. Priest, commander of the Denver Police Department's Major Crimes Section, states that the mere existence of the videotaped confession causes defense attorneys to plead cases more often.[12] The ability to show a judge, defense attorney, and jury the suspect being interrogated can prevent defense allegations of coercion, illegitimate handling of the suspect, or inadmissibility of a confession as a result of Miranda rights not being read. The videotape allows the judge, defense attorney, and jury to hear the suspect's own words, view his or her mannerisms, and observe the interaction between the suspect and detective. The traditional method of the detective going on the stand to give a play-by-play of the interrogation and engaging in a battle of "he said, she said" is virtually eliminated when interrogations are videotaped. That interplay is now available for the court to see and hear, and can reduce investigator time and cross-examination of the detective in court.

---

12. Priest, Jonathyn W. Homicide Investigations Conference. Washington, D.C.: Police Executive Research Forum, 2006.

Direct Observation

Departments that videotape interrogations highlight the power it has on juries to be able to *see* the interview for themselves. There have been eye-opening cases of the videotape capturing much more than just the detective-suspect interaction. Some suspects have incriminated themselves and clearly contradicted their own defense while on videotape in custodial settings. Examples include the following:

- In Hennepin County, Minnesota, a suspect claimed that his blindness prohibited him from being able to commit the offense. While taping, the detectives left the room and the suspect proceeded to pick up the newspaper and read it, not knowing or forgetting that the videotape was recording his actions.

- In a case from the Kankakee County, Illinois, Sheriff's Department, a man repeatedly denied his involvement in a rape and stabbing which left a woman dead, yet he sang, "Ding, dong, the witch is dead" when detectives left the room and he forgot that the camera was rolling. Although not a clear admission of guilt, this was still an interesting development for the jury to see in evaluating his behavior and overall attitude.

- One suspect changed his story five times while acting the crime out, aiding the prosecution in rendering his testimony as less than truthful.

- A youth's father accompanied him in the interrogation room. He asked his son if there were any witnesses to the crime. His son responded, "No, we killed them all."

Direct observation eliminates concern about the accuracy of unrecorded interview statements. The accuracy of videotaped interviews and interrogations is superior to notes and secondhand recall. These older methods, and even an audio recording, can be error-prone and open to interpretation. The videotape removes the element of doubt. Jurors not only hear what suspects say, they see them saying it. The videotaped interview accurately documents the suspect's description of events, admissions, denials, and/or confession. The videotape also prevents suspects and witnesses from changing statements or denying they made statements at a later date.

Further, direct observation offers the judge and jury a greater ability to evaluate a suspect's intent. Intent is clearer in a video recording than it is in other types of recall and audio recording. Hearing the inflection in the suspect's voice, his certainty in what he is saying, and his repeated admissions or rejections of information can help jurors evaluate his credibility. The suspect's physical mannerisms and emotional state while speaking are essential to help a jury interpret the validity of a person's statements. Jurors are more likely to believe a confession if they see corroborating information presented and do not see coercive tactics.

Review and Training

An advantage of video recording is that detectives can view them repeatedly to identify details they may have missed initially. Supervisors can review the videotapes for quality control and training practices. And even after the trial is over, a videotape may be useful in the appeals process. Appeals no longer hinge on the detective's recall and notes; the power of the testimony remains in each repeated viewing. Videotapes can also be powerful training tools for new investigators and for preserving the institutional knowledge of seasoned homicide detectives.

CONCERNS ABOUT VIDEOTAPING INTERROGATIONS

Not all police departments share this support for videotaping and are concerned that its use by other departments will force them to adopt the technology. Some departments have such strong concerns about its benefits that they do not videotape any portion of interviews or interrogations. Others believe that videotaping is beneficial only in certain circumstances, such as a suspect's final statement or confession.

Given that no empirical evidence supports the premise that videotaping helps close cases and secure convictions, departments are reluctant to change their investigative procedures. The most frequently mentioned concerns with videotaping include the following:

1. Reluctance to reveal investigative tactics, including deceiving suspects, which may create negative perception among community members.

One Department's Approach to Videotaping: Denver Police Department

The Denver Police Department has a Standard Operating Procedure and *Training Bulletin*[13] for videotaping interrogations and using the video rooms (see Appendix E). The *Training Bulletin* describes factors that detectives can capture in a recording, including clothing worn by the suspect, demeanor and actions, injuries (or lack of injuries), body language, eye movement and other nonverbal gestures, and mental and physical condition. The video interrogation room is simple in appearance. It allows for complete videotaping of the interrogation, as well as recording of all activity displayed on what is called a SMART Board. This interactive device allows detectives to display crime scene photographs, drawings, wound diagrams, photo lineups, video streams, vehicle photographs, and much more. The images and edits are saved electronically and captured on videotape. The room also allows for instant communication between detectives and commanders outside of the video room via the computer that sits in front of the detective conducting the interrogation (see Figure 5). ■

Figure 5. Denver Police Department, Video Interview Room #1

---

13. Priest, Jonathyn W. Video Interview Facility, Video Interview Techniques, *Training Bulletin*. Denver Police Department, Crimes Against Persons Bureau, 2006.

2. A belief that video recording decreases suspect cooperation.

3. Questions of legality and consent issues.

4. Concerns about costs.

5. A belief that video recording might lead departments to become overly dependent on technology.

Erosion of Public Trust

Concern about public scrutiny of police tactics is perhaps the most often cited deterrent to videotaping. Departments assert that videotaping will give juries and the public the opportunity to scrutinize the investigative process, the legitimate tactics that are allowable within interrogation environments, and the professional integrity of an individual detective or the entire department.

Departments that have adopted videotaping agree that these are legitimate concerns that need to be considered carefully. An official from one department said, "It's hard to have a jury trust a detective who has just taken an oath to tell the truth, yet see him lying on the videotape in an attempt to trick or confuse." An official from another department said that its prosecutors discourage lying on videotape because of the negative consequences it can have on a jury. Aside from lying, officials fear that other legitimate tactics to trick or confuse a suspect, when captured on videotape, will convey a negative image of investigators and the department. Further, police officials fear that some detectives, regardless of their effectiveness, may not make a positive impression on the video and might harm the citizens' perception of the department.

Officials from some departments that do not videotape argue that videotaping interrogations should not be used as a means to build community trust. They believe that the interrogation of suspects is too important to be compromised by videotaping, especially without scientific evidence demonstrating its benefits. They say that other efforts, such as strong community policing initiatives, should be used to build community trust in the department.

Some departments are reluctant to videotape because they believe there will always be skeptics on a jury who will ask, "But what happened *before* the videotape began recording?" Officials in these departments point out that, if the skeptics have their way, officers will eventually have to videotape every second of every encounter with suspects. Rather than be forced into such an untenable position, they choose not to use videotaping.

Decreased Cooperation

Another concern that departments cite is the possibility that suspects will "clam up" if they know they are being videotaped. They reject claims that suspects talk freely on videotape; rather, they say, the knowledge that one is being videotaped causes people to be reticent and guarded in their comments.

Consent

Gaining consent from suspects or witnesses can be an obstacle to videotaping. States typically require single- or dual-party consent to videotaping. In a single-party consent state, investigators do not have to alert the suspect that he is being videotaped, although many do so nevertheless. In a dual-party consent state, a suspect can refuse to be videotaped.

Some prosecutors are concerned that "a reasonable expectation of privacy," a federal constitutional doctrine, bars the videotaping of interrogations without consent. Geller (1993), however, points out that the federal doctrine does not pertain to station house interrogations. State and local laws may prohibit videotaping though, without dual-party consent, and departments are encouraged to discuss these concerns with their local prosecutors before implementing videotaping procedures.

Cost

Departments have a variety of questions and concerns about the sophistication of the equipment, and how extensively it must be installed in interview rooms or any other facilities where suspects might be questioned or observed. Reiterating the concern that every encounter with a suspect might have to be videotaped, department officials fear that the entire station house would have to be wired for videotaping around the clock. Justifying these costs in the face of scarce municipal resources, especially for agencies with multiple facilities, can be difficult.

Technology Complexity and Dependence

Another concern about videotaping interrogations is with the recording technology and how it may alter police procedures. Police officials point out that the technology may become so complex that it requires special training for investigators or even a dedicated support staff to keep the cameras and other equipment operating. And if recording equipment malfunctions during an interrogation, investigators might have to interrupt their questioning or even start over. The safeguarding of recordings against loss or tampering requires new policies and procedures, and possibly storage facilities. Officials also fear that an over-reliance on videotaping may, over time, erode investigators' ability to document their interrogations through careful and comprehensive note-taking.

So, Should Departments Videotape?

Every agency should consider the above concerns before implementing videotape interrogations or expanding its use. A key concern for nearly every department is that videotaped interrogations or interviews could somehow harm or embarrass investigators, especially when shown in court. And while there have been situations where these fears were realized, training and familiarity with the system have, in many cases, eliminated those problems. Indeed, many maintain that their interrogation tactics have been enhanced as a result of videotape training. One sergeant from Minneapolis said, "It has not changed the way [the detectives] do their interviews, but has proven that our interview techniques are sound."

Increasingly, courts are requesting and encouraging videotaped interrogations. They are often unsympathetic to departments that fail to furnish a videotaped interrogation. Sullivan highlights a case where the Drug Enforcement Administration failed to videotape an interrogation, although they are permitted to use video recording, and the delivery of Miranda warnings was in question. The judge said, "Affording the court the benefit of watching or listening to a videotaped or audiotaped statement is invaluable; indeed, a tape-recorded interrogation allows the court to more accurately assess whether a statement was given knowingly, voluntarily, and intelligently. Taping is thus the only means of eliminating 'swearing contests' about what went on in the interrogation room."[14]

Due to the increasing demand for and expectation of videotaped interrogations, a number of states, including Massachusetts and New Jersey, require that if interrogations are *not* recorded, the jury must receive special instructions notifying them of the lack of a videotape, and to consider confessions with caution.

AGENCY CONSIDERATIONS FOR VIDEOTAPING INTERROGATIONS

Departments need to consider a number of variables to assess current videotaping protocols or the need to videotape at all. This list is not exhaustive, but does include those variables highlighted as important throughout discussions with departments across the country.

Necessity

What are the benefits and disadvantages of a department's current interrogation recording protocol? Is there a need for the department to modify its current protocols? If so, what is the need and how can it be met? As a department decides whether to adopt videotaping it may be important to take into consideration how many interrogations its does each month or each year. Consulting with other departments, including some that use video recording and others that do not, can help agencies determine the most appropriate policies.

Current Regulations

Are there current state or local mandates that could affect a decision about videotaping interrogations? Are bills pending? State and local mandates have driven several departments across the United States and internationally to videotape interrogations. It is essential that a department remains aware of laws that potentially could change the way in which it carries out investigations. Some departments that have adopted

---

[14]. Sullivan, T. *Police Experiences with Recording Custodial Interrogations.* Northwestern University School of Law, Center on Wrongful Convictions. Special Report, 2004.

videotaping cited the possibility of a legislative mandate as the reason for their decision. They believed that voluntarily adopting videotaping allowed them to do it in a manner consistent with existing agency protocols and at their own pace, and that it is better to do it voluntarily than have it forced on them. By voluntarily adopting videotaping, departments have a claim to the moral high ground and gain recognition for that, which they would not have if forced by outsiders to videotape interrogations.

The Decision

What steps need to be taken to make the decision whether or not to videotape interrogations? Departments should involve all key stakeholders, especially the local prosecutor, and all affected groups (detectives and technological staff) in evaluating and/or developing the protocols. One department cautioned others to consider the challenges they will face if they adopt videotaping but then decide to rescind that decision.

Policy

What portions of the interrogation will a department want to record? What crimes will be open to videotaped interrogations? Where will videotaping take place? How will confessions in the squad car be recognized in light of the fact that other interrogations are videotaped at the station? In addition, will the department have specific policies on the videotaped interrogations of juveniles, non-English speakers, and other vulnerable populations? It is important that a department document its rationale for choosing to videotape some and not all people, videotaping only certain portions of the interrogation, or videotaping only in cases involving certain types of crimes. As noted earlier, some judges are becoming unsympathetic to departments that fail to produce a taped interrogation. A firm and rational policy may assist the department in defending its decisions. For departments that choose not to videotape interrogations, it is important that they are able to support their decision.

Logistics

What equipment will be needed and how much will it cost? As noted previously, departments sometimes cite price as an obstacle to videotaping interrogations. Departments that have adopted videotaping say that the price is minimal compared to the huge settlements that result from wrongful convictions—a consideration that is driving some states to videotape. Price, nonetheless, is a consideration. Minimally, departments would need a video camera and a location for taping and videotape storage, or a digital video camera and a computer for storing the electronic data. Other logistical considerations include placement of the camera in the room and who is on screen, and assigning someone the task of storing the evidence and ensuring that the recording protocol is adhered to.

Training Implications

How does the potential change in policy and procedure affect training requirements? Will technical staff need to assist detectives in carrying out videotaping? Departments may need to develop or revise their policies and procedures to incorporate changes in the collection and storage of electronic evidence. If a department is new to videotaping, it must recognize the reluctance of some detectives to be on camera or have their work openly available for scrutiny, and may need to develop a training program to acclimate those involved.

Departmental Mindset

Officials should assess the current perception of videotaping in their departments. What are the perceived benefits and pitfalls? Along with considerations noted in the training implications mentioned above, departments need to support detectives as they transition into videotaped interrogations by allowing them to identify the benefits and challenges for themselves.

CONCLUSION

Videotaping can be a valuable tool for law enforcement agencies. Many departments do it, but not all use it the same way or in the same situations. Departments that videotape seemingly are satisfied with the benefits they believe are a result of videotaped interrogations. On the other hand, departments that do not videotape, or do so only in limited situations, express concern that videotaping may be more of a hindrance than a help.

What most departments agree on, however, is the need for empirical data that show the measurable outcomes of videotaping, specifically on the impact of confessions, clearance rates, and convictions. Such data would allow departments to obtain the support necessary to implement video interrogations or revise policies accordingly. This research should include pilot studies in law enforcement agencies, to provide realistic settings, procedures, and outcomes.

6

DNA, Crime Labs, and Law Enforcement

> "...DNA does more than just identify the source of the sample; it can place a known individual at a crime scene, in a home, or in a room where the suspect claimed not to have been. It can refute a claim of self-defense and put a weapon in the suspect's hand. It can change a story from an alibi to one of consent. The more officers know how to use DNA, the more powerful tool it becomes."
>
> NATIONAL COMMISSION ON THE
> FUTURE OF DNA EVIDENCE (1999)[1]

IN THE LAST DECADE, DEOXYRIBONUCLEIC ACID (DNA) HAS assumed a prominent role in homicide investigations. It has proved to be a highly valuable tool in identifying potential suspects and has helped the criminal justice system recognize its mistakes in convicting innocent people. As the justice system has found ever-increasing ways to put DNA technology to use, the number and size of public and private forensic labs has increased.

This new emphasis on DNA, as beneficial as it is, imposes costs on the justice system. The time burden on law enforcement and forensic analysts is enormous. Lab personnel continue to report significant backlogs of cases and a shortage of trained lab professionals. One example is

---

[1]. *What Every Law Enforcement Officer Should Know About DNA Evidence.* Washington, D.C.: U.S. Department of Justice, National Institute of Justice, National Commission on the Future of DNA Evidence, 1999. www.ncjrs.gov/pdffiles1/nij/bc000614.pdf

the nationwide adoption of legislation to collect and submit convicted offenders' DNA to a national database. The collection and submission of offenders' DNA samples and resulting investigations related to this effort often fall to law enforcement. This is in addition to their already active investigations and cold case reviews.

Publicity about advances in DNA technology has also fostered an unrealistic expectation among laypeople about the availability of forensic evidence and analysis in the courtroom. There are ample examples of the "CSI Effect," named for the television programs that feature the latest advances in criminal forensic technology, hindering the prosecution of cases because the jury believed that more forensic evidence should have been available or analyzed.

The challenges associated with DNA are extensive, but so are the benefits. This chapter discusses the role of DNA in homicide investigations, the surge in DNA forensics, the relationships between crime labs and police departments, and policy considerations regarding the use of DNA in homicide investigations. DNA testing is an enormous topic with wide-ranging implications; the particular issues discussed in this chapter are ones cited by law enforcement officials as among the most pressing and difficult when they convened at PERF's "Promoting Effective Homicide Investigations" conference in May 2006.

DEOXYRIBONUCLEIC ACID (DNA)

DNA is a powerful tool for law enforcement in the identification of possible suspects. DNA and other forensic evidence may be able to identify who was at or near a crime scene or was with the victim at some point, but it may not necessarily identify the guilty party. Investigators still must rigorously investigate cases and evaluate forensic and other evidence to understand exactly what transpired.

Background

In 1987, Dr. Alec Jeffreys coined the phrase "DNA fingerprinting." In England in November 1987, Robert Melias was the first person convicted of a crime (rape) on the basis of DNA. The first U.S. conviction was also in November 1987, in Orange County, Florida, where Tommy Andrews was convicted of rape after his DNA, taken from a blood sample, matched semen traces taken from the victim. Since that time, DNA has been accepted as evidence in U.S. courts.

Since the inception of DNA fingerprinting, detectives have been very creative in the ways in which they collect samples for analysis. A number of homicides have been solved using saliva from a sealed envelope. Extraordinary cases include the following:

- A suspect's DNA was taken from saliva in a dental impression mold and then matched with the DNA swabbed from a victim's bite mark.[2]

- A masked rapist was convicted of forced oral copulation when his victim's DNA matched bodily fluids swabbed from the suspect's penis 6 hours after the offense.[3]

- While surveilling a suspect, officers saw him spit on the street. One officer used a napkin to collect the spittle. The saliva provided enough evidence to charge the man with the sexual assault and robbery of two female victims.[4]

- In 2003, nearly 30 years after the crime and through DNA analysis, a man was found guilty of the 1974 rape and homicide of a 19-year-old pregnant woman.[5]

DNA's Contributions

DNA has been used to help prosecute guilty parties and exonerate the innocent for nearly 2 decades. The 50 largest crime labs in the country received more than 30,000 requests for DNA testing in 2004, according to the Bureau of Justice Statistics. And since 1984, DNA has been instrumental in exonerating 205 persons (see Figure 6). Further, in more than 35 percent of those exonerated cases, the true culprits have been identified.[6] Many more innocent people have avoided convictions as a result

---

2. President's DNA Initiative. (2003). http://www.dna.gov/audiences/investigators/know/whatisdna
3. Connors, Edward et al. *Convicted by Juries, Exonerated by Science: Case Studies in the Use of DNA Evidence to Establish Innocence After Trial*. Washington, D.C.: U.S. Department of Justice, June 1996.
4. President's DNA Initiative. (2003). http://dnacourses.dna.gov/letraining_adv/Sources LocationsLimitations/SalivaExample
5. Starrs, J. "The CSI Effect." *Scientific Sleuthing Review*, Vol. 28 (3)(2004).
6. *Innocence Project Case Profiles*. The Innocence Project, no date. http://www.innocence project.org/know/

of not matching specific forensic evidence left by the actual perpetrator. The National Institute of Justice reports that approximately 25 percent of primary suspects in sexual assaults are excluded when DNA tests are conducted.[7]

DNA in Demand: Cases and Backlogs

To some extent, DNA analysis has been a victim of its own success. The number of samples submitted to labs increases each year. And, while labs have been able to increase their personnel and analytical capabilities to keep pace with the submissions, it now appears that many DNA laboratories in the United States and Canada are facing an overwhelming backlog of samples, causing them to miss targeted turnaround times. Compounding the problem are shortages in funding, crime lab staffs, detectives available to work the cases and prosecutors to take the cases to trial. Because of the interrelatedness of investigation, analysis and prosecution, an increase in demand for any one of the components can overburden the other two components (see Figure 7).

Figure 6. **DNA Exonerations by Year**[8]

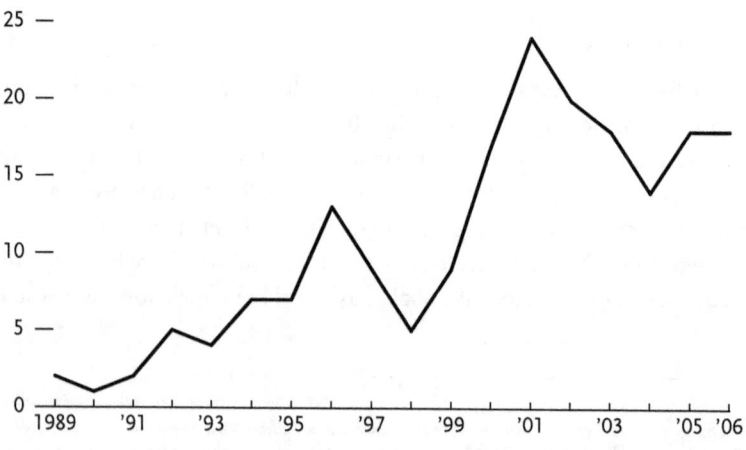

---

7. Connors, Edward et al. *Convicted by Juries, Exonerated by Science: Case Studies in the Use of DNA Evidence to Establish Innocence After Trial.* Washington, D.C.: U.S. Department of Justice, June 1996.
8. Chart modeled after data and similar chart from The Innocence Project, 2006. http://www.witnesstoinnocence.org/facts.htm

For some departments, the DNA case backlog is in the thousands (see sidebar on page 90 for a discussion of the Houston Crime Lab). Caseloads are high because they include active cases, cold cases, and cases that were closed but reopened because of additional analysis or evidence. DNA is collected from crime scenes, from thousands of convicted offenders, and at the request of medical examiners, police, attorneys, and other interested persons who believe DNA testing can help them prove their cases or otherwise give them useful information. The number of cases in which DNA analysis was conducted tripled from 1997 to 2000.

Backlogs are especially severe regarding the critical cases known as "subject cases," in which suspects have been identified, so DNA testing could play an important role in bolstering the case or exonerating any false suspects. In 1999, labs reported receiving 21,000 subject cases. One year later, subject case submissions increased by nearly 50 percent to 31,000. Subject case backlogs have increased by 135 percent from 1997 to 2000, even though convicted offender backlogs (those samples routinely collected from convicted offenders) decreased by 7 percent. Still, the

Figure 7. **Backlog Cycle and Requirements for Funding: A Comprehensive Approach**

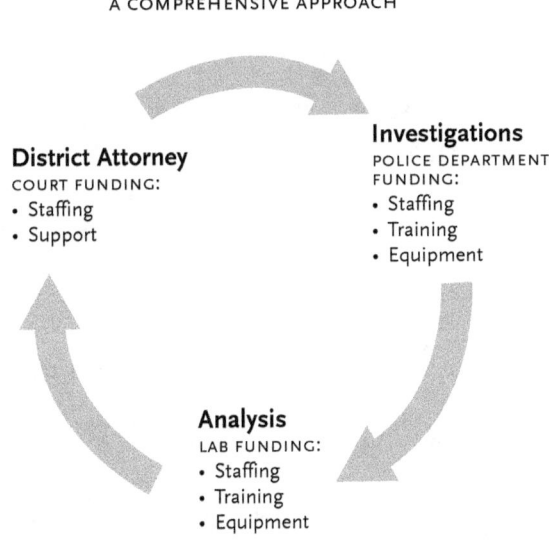

National Institute of Justice estimated in 2003 that the convicted offender samples that remained untested numbered between 200,000 and 300,000.[9] In addition to those samples collected but not analyzed, another important category is DNA samples that have not yet been collected. Between 500,000 and 1,000,000 samples still needed to be collected from convicted offenders as a result of state legislation requiring convicted offenders' DNA.[10]

The Bureau of Justice Statistics surveyed the 50 largest crime labs in the country[11] and learned that the 2002 end-of-year backlog for all analyses was more than double the number at the beginning of the year (see Table 4). Cases involving DNA analysis accounted for 10 to 15 percent of the overall backlog in 2002, yet they accounted for approximately 2 percent of both requests and completed requests.

Lab directors often tout their ability to turn around a DNA analysis within a few days. Unless the analysis receives the highest priority, however, investigators in the typical homicide case are likely to wait several months and perhaps up to a year or more for analysis. As a result, in 2000, 45 percent of state- and locally-run crime labs reported that they contracted out to private labs to help reduce their backlogs.[12]

Table 4. **Crime Lab Backlogs**

	2002 Year-Start Backlog	Requests	Requests Completed	2002 Year-End Backlog
Overall Cases	116,707	1,204,922	1,051,302	270,327
DNA	18,130	30,761	18,171	30,720

9. President's DNA Initiative. (2003). www.dna.gov.
10. *Advancing Justice Through DNA Technology: Using DNA to Solve Crimes*, U.S. Department of Justice, March 2003, http://www.usdoj.gov/ag/dnapolicybook_cov.htm.
11. Hickman, Matthew, J. and Joseph L. Petersen. *50 Largest Crime Labs, 2000*. Bureau of Justice Statistics Fact Sheet. NCJ # 205988. Washington, D.C.: U.S. Department of Justice, Bureau of Justice Statistics, September 2004.
12. Steadman, Greg W. *Survey of DNA Crime Laboratories, 2001*. Bureau of Justice Statistics Bulletin. NCJ #191191. Washington, D.C.: U.S. Department of Justice, Bureau of Justice Statistics, January 2002.

DNA EVIDENCE IN LAW ENFORCEMENT AGENCIES

Law enforcement agencies rely on various arrangements to ensure the analysis of DNA and other forensic evidence. Many large departments have their own labs while others rely on local, state, federal or private labs. For example, three departments are highlighted below (Table 5) to include details of which lab they use; their average turnaround time for DNA analysis; and what, if any, future plans might exist.

In an attempt to increase forensic capabilities, many law enforcement agencies are exploring the feasibility of starting their own DNA lab. Creating and operating a forensics laboratory is a complex task, and departments must carefully examine the potential challenges and benefits. Among the issues to consider are the following:

- Staffing and credentialing
- Oversight
- Evidence management and prioritization
- DNA in the courtroom

Table 5. **Police Departments, Labs, and DNA Turnarounds: Three Examples**

City (Population)	Lab Utilization	Typical DNA Turnaround*	Future Plans
Washington, D.C. PD (550,000)	Federal	1 year	Secure own lab
Denver PD (557,900)	Own (~35 staff)	3 months	$20-million upgrade to new lab with 60,000 sq. ft.
San Jose PD (912,300)	County Lab (shared by 14 police depts.)	6–8 weeks	New county facility; expand space by 2/3

*A typical turnaround is defined as a non-high profile case and the reported current expected time necessary for turnaround.

- Funding
- Other resources.

This section of the chapter highlights these considerations and includes key points to consider when evaluating departmental lab capabilities, accessibilities, and outcomes.

Staffing and Credentials

Forensic labs require highly proficient and credentialed personnel, from the director to analysts and technicians. One of the most often-cited reasons for starting a lab is the need for shorter turnaround times for analysis, accompanied by greater access to lab staff. For many departments, especially large ones with heavy caseloads, this is a compelling reason. Delays of months or even years in the analysis of forensic evidence can have a significant impact on the department's ability to solve cases and bring offenders to justice. A dedicated lab can certainly reduce those delays.

Forensic labs are facing a significant shortfall in credentialed analysts. Labs across the country collectively reported that they would need nearly 2,000 additional full-time personnel to achieve a 30-day turnaround for requests to analyze samples.[13] The cost for this personnel demand was estimated at $70 million. This understaffing creates bottlenecks in processing and analysis that, in turn, slows investigations. Indeed, the shortage is so significant in some parts of the country that departments are bidding against each to hire and retain forensic specialists.

Oversight

Another issue to consider is the relationship between investigators and forensic analysts, who, although they work for the same department, must adhere to their specific roles and responsibilities. Analysts must be able to perform analyses and interpret results consistent with scientific standards and free of any potential persuasion or influence. Departments

---

13. Federal Bureau of Investigation. CODIS. http://www.fbi.gov/hq/lab/fsc/backissu/oct2005/research/2005_10_research02.htm

must think carefully about organizational relationships and reporting authorities, to ensure that work is completed in a way that allows the department to remain effective while operating with the highest degree of integrity. Some law enforcement leaders have been adamant that labs need to be completely independent of departments for integrity purposes. On the other hand, if a crime lab is within the police department's authority, the department must ensure adequate oversight of the lab and its staff.

Both independent and department-affiliated labs have been criticized for a lack of standards, poor oversight, and mishandling or misrepresenting of facts to bias a case. One of the most notorious cases of faulty forensic work and testimony involved Fred Zain, a serologist with the West Virginia State Police Crime Laboratory and then the Bexar County, Texas, Medical Examiner's office. Mr. Zain falsely reported evidence as conclusive, altered lab records, and overstated the strength of results. These behaviors were not only illegal but highly unethical and jeopardized the entire justice system. The West Virginia State Supreme Court ruled that none of the testimony Mr. Zain gave in more than 130 cases was credible. Further, the Court ordered him indicted for perjury.[14] This is the exception, but officials need to be mindful of the importance of supervision and maintaining high ethical standards.

Evidence Management and Prioritization

A crime scene can yield dozens of samples for forensic analysis. And while investigators, crime scene technicians, and forensic analysts contribute to the prosecution of an offender, their methods and priorities are sometimes different. The recent advances in DNA capabilities have highlighted these differences. Department administrators must carefully consider who will have responsibility for identifying, collecting, transporting and storing DNA evidence. Investigators, laboratory personnel and evidence technicians should work together to determine the most effective procedures for managing evidence. Those procedures must be delineated in written policies. Similarly, personnel must receive training

---

[14] National Institute of Justice. *Convicted by Juries, Exonerated by Science: Case Studies in the Use of DNA Evidence to Establish Innocence After Trial.* Washington, D.C.: U.S. Department of Justice, National Institute of Justice, 1996.

The Fall and Rise of One Crime Lab

"[Houston has] become the Enron of crime labs..."
DAVID BERG, HOUSTON TRIAL LAWYER[15]

In 2002, a local television station investigated the Houston Police Department's (HPD) Crime Lab procedures and outcomes, spurring a long, expensive, and painful journey for the lab. As a result of the investigation, an independent investigator, Michael Bromwich, was brought in by the new police chief, Harold Hurtt, and was assigned three main tasks: 1. examine policies and procedures guiding the lab; 2. evaluate more than 2,000 case samples that were processed at the lab between 1987 and 2002; and 3. closely examine individual cases where defendants were convicted using samples that were found to have major flaws during that time period. His findings uncovered unqualified and poorly trained lab staff, poor lab oversight and management, "major errors" that included a failure to test essential samples, inaccurate results, misrepresentation of results, contamination of evidence, and falsifying reported results.[16]

More than 30 percent of the DNA samples retested yielded major errors. The DNA lab was shut down in 2002 as a result of these findings. During that time, DNA evidence was sent to private labs for testing.

The aftermath resulted in several lab employees being implicated for most of the erroneous findings; two prisoners being exonerated; four death-row inmates' lab results being placed in serious question; a projected cost of more than $10 million;[17] and the huge challenge

---

15. Dole, L., T. Wilson, and K. Walsh. *Houston Crime Lab's Fake Results May Undermine Prosecutors.* (No date) www.dydflaw.com/index.cfm?t=11&la=209
16. Bromwich, M.R. *Fifth Report of the Independent Investigator for the Houston Police Department Crime Laboratory and Property Room.* May 11, 2006. www.hpdlabinvestigation.org
17. Nichols, B. (2006, February 22). Response to crime lab scandal criticized. Retrieved June 30, 2006 from www.khou.com

associated with restoring the integrity of the lab and ensuring sound findings. In addition to the Bromwich investigations, two grand juries investigated the lab staff and procedures, but did not return any criminal indictments.

The challenge to restore the lab's integrity has been under way since the investigation began. Chief Hurtt has taken a number of major steps. A new lab director and DNA division chief were hired and have secured accreditation for the entire lab, including the DNA division. The American Society of Crime Lab Directors and Bromwich himself have recognized the effort Houston has made to instill confidence in the lab. The battle is far from over, and lessons were learned the hard way; but this experience highlights the importance of competent staff, training, protocols, oversight, and quality assurance to deliver accurate outcomes. This is a lesson that can benefit all labs and police departments. ∎

on these procedures and their roles, as well as on advances in DNA technology. A number of departments now provide investigators with an annual in-service class focusing on DNA technology and its effect on investigations.

Detectives need to be well-versed in processing crime scenes so they can effectively identify and collect DNA evidence or oversee evidence technicians as they process scenes. Just like there are differences in levels of competence among homicide detectives, the same is true of evidence technicians. Agencies get only one chance to process a scene properly, so those personnel who have those responsibilities must know the proper procedures, including the most common items of evidence that may contain DNA, the location of the DNA on those items, and the proper procedures for collecting it.

A common tendency among investigators and crime scene technicians is to collect as much evidence as possible, with the assumption that the analysis will determine whether the evidence is important to the case. From an investigator's perspective, this practice makes sense. But from an analyst's perspective, this can contribute to an already heavy workload, and may not be the most efficient use of an analyst's time. Again, proper training should be provided that instructs investigators and technicians in the amount and type of evidence to collect. Some of the basic principles of collecting DNA evidence include the following:[18]

- Wear gloves. Change them between handling different samples of evidence.

- Use disposable instruments or clean them thoroughly before and after handling each sample.

- Do not touch the area where you believe DNA may exist.

- Do not talk, sneeze, and cough over evidence.

- Do not touch your face, nose, and mouth when collecting and packaging evidence.

---

[18]. *What Every Law Enforcement Officer Should Know About DNA Evidence.* Washington, D.C.: National Commission on the Future of DNA Evidence, National Institute of Justice, September 1999.

- Air-dry evidence

- Put dry evidence into new paper bags or envelopes; do not use plastic bags.

- Do not use staples.

- If repackaging of evidence is necessary, consult with laboratory personnel.

Storing and preserving evidence creates a number of challenges, as well. As DNA technology continues to advance, evidence once believed to be unable to yield usable DNA can become important for analysis years later. Careful storage and preservation of evidence is vital, and agencies need to develop appropriate protocols that will preserve DNA evidence.

A comprehensive report published in 2004 found that the many law enforcement agencies "misunderstand" the benefits of DNA testing; that is, 25 percent of the surveyed agencies stated that they did not send DNA evidence to a crime lab because they had not identified a suspect, a situation when DNA evidence could actually prove quite useful.[19] Educating investigators about the uses and benefits of DNA will reduce the backlog in crime labs and will result in a greater number of solved cases. The President's DNA Initiative provides online courses for law enforcement officers. These courses can be found at http://dna.gov/training/letraining/. In addition, a variety of publications and brochures are available for investigators through the President's DNA Initiative at http://www.dna.gov/pubs/investigators/.

An abundance of evidence samples can create problems for analysts who must prioritize and manage this workload. Absent any guidance from investigators about the relative importance of evidence samples, laboratory staff may prioritize samples in a number of ways:

- Case court dates

- Prosecutor requests

---

[19]. Lovrich, N. P., T. C. Pratt, M. J. Gaffney, C. L. Johnson, and C. H. Asplen. *National Forensic DNA Study, Final Report*. February 2004. http://www.ncjrs.gov/pdffiles1/nij/grants/203970.pdf

- High profile cases
- In order of receipt.

Creating an objective chart detailing how cases should be prioritized will create a standard procedure that will aid in reducing backlogs.

The National Commission on the Future of DNA Evidence recommended, and a number of lab staff and detectives have agreed, that the key to appropriate prioritization and reduced turnaround times is maintaining a positive relationship between investigators and analysts. If detectives and analysts can discuss the samples collected, questions that the detectives need to have answered, and the possible usefulness of the samples collected, lab staff will be better prepared to prioritize samples for analysis.

In much the same way that investigators follow case management protocols, the efficient management of DNA samples would benefit from protocols developed jointly by investigators and analysts. Agencies need to consider the needs of investigators and analysts to ensure that investigators have the evidence they need without overwhelming analysts with unnecessary samples.

DNA in the Courtroom: "The CSI Effect"

The "CSI Effect," named for the popular *CSI* television shows, refers to people's unrealistically high expectations about the power of forensic evidence. One frequently cited example of the "CSI Effect" is the layperson's notion that fingerprints "should" appear on any object. Another example is a case where a jury acquitted a defendant because of the detective's failure to test a soda bottle at the crime scene for DNA evidence.[20]

Juries may find it hard to accept that real-life investigations are very different from those seen on television. Further, each police department is different and has a different level of access to crime labs that may or may not have the latest technology. Each crime scene is different. Often evidence has degraded or cannot be tested for other reasons. Even if

---

20. Starrs, J. "The CSI Effect." *Scientific Sleuthing Review*, Vol. 28 (3)(2004).

potentially useful evidence is found at a crime scene, enormous backlogs at the crime lab may delay its testing for many months, unlike the scenes in *CSI*, where test results are given within minutes.

To counter the CSI Effect, departments have moved toward the use of "negative evidence witnesses," who educate the jury and judge on the evidence that was available, collected, and analyzed in the particular case. They can also assist the jury in understanding why particular evidence (e.g., a fingerprint on the weapon) was *not* found at the crime scene in the case.

Funding

Crime lab budgets have increased for the most part; however, some remain constrained, given the backlog and the enormous importance of DNA testing in the exoneration of innocent people and conviction of those who are guilty. The mean annual budget for the 50 largest DNA labs in 2000 was $464,000.[21] The mean annual budget for forensics labs in general in 2000 was $3,091,000. Using these figures, DNA budgets accounts for 15 percent of the entire lab budget annually.

Recognizing the importance of DNA advances, the National Institute of Justice began funding labs in 2001—specifically to reduce backlogs—through the Forensic Casework DNA Backlog Reduction Program and the Convicted Offender DNA Backlog Reduction Programs. Another initiative, the Solving Cold Cases with DNA grant program, awarded 38 proposals totaling more than $14 million.[22]

In addition, two sizable funding sources include assistance for various aspects of building and maintaining crime labs. They are the Paul Coverdell Forensic Services Improvement Grant and the President's DNA Initiative.

The Paul Coverdell Forensic Science Improvement grant program provides funding to crime laboratories for laboratory facilities, personnel, equipment, computerization, supplies, accreditation, certification, and education and training.

---

21. Federal Bureau of Investigation. CODIS. Retrieved October 5, 2006, from http://www.fbi.gov.
22. U.S. Department of Justice. Office of Justice Programs. http://www.ojp.usdoj.gov/funding/

In 2003, President Bush announced a 5-year, more than $1 billion DNA initiative to improve the use of DNA in the criminal justice system.[23] The President's DNA Initiative aims to do the following:

- Eliminate the backlog of cases
- Improve lab capacities;
- Stimulate research
- Develop training;
- Provide post-conviction DNA access
- Ensure DNA technology is used for missing persons cases
- Protect the innocent.

In 2005 and 2006, Congress appropriated more than $100 million to fund activities under the President's DNA Initiative.

Other Resources: Combined DNA Index System (CODIS)

The Combined DNA Index System (CODIS) is a free database that local and state law enforcement agencies can use to exchange and compare DNA information electronically. It is a resource for matching DNA in a series of crimes, even if they are years apart. The database is hosted by the Federal Bureau of Investigation and has been in existence since 1990. CODIS' participating laboratories are located in all 50 states and operate at the local, state, and national level. The database is divided into three tiers: the Local DNA Index System (LDIS), the State DNA Index System (SDIS), and the National DNA Index System (NDIS). This structure allows each agency to operate the database within its jurisdiction's legal framework. More than 170 public law enforcement laboratories in the United States use NDIS, and internationally 40 departments in 25 countries use the CODIS software.

---

23. President's DNA Initiative. (2003). www.dna.gov.

As of May 2007, CODIS contained more than 4.7 million DNA profiles. The profiles are broken up into forensic profiles, where the DNA originated from crime scene evidence, and offender profiles, which contain the DNA of individuals convicted of sex offenses and other violent crimes. About 4.5 million profiles in the database are offender profiles. The CODIS system will identify matches between forensic DNA evidence and DNA from offenders. The CODIS system may also contain DNA profiles of missing persons, unidentified human remains, and arrestees (if state law allows).

As it has already assisted in more than 50,000 investigations, resulting in more than 49,000 matches, CODIS is becoming an important tool for law enforcement. Because the system electronically matches DNA evidence to a growing list of convicted offenders, law enforcement agencies across jurisdictions can rely on the system to catch serial offenders.[24]

CONSIDERATIONS FOR DNA AND FORENSIC LABS

The challenges identified in this chapter are threefold:

1. Promote a greater understanding of the potential of DNA

2. Support multidimensional funding of labs, police, support agencies, and prosecutors to comprehensively work the cases that result from the advancements in DNA analysis and to reduce the backlogs

3. Foster a balanced relationship between labs and police to ensure greater case management of evidence and open communication.

A department's decision to start its own lab, instead of using state, federal, or private facilities, is a significant change that requires thorough consideration of all possible implications. Departments need to carefully evaluate their current lab facilities and their future needs. Considerations include: financial resources, facilities, and equipment; workload demands and trends; training and staffing needs; and working relationships among investigators, analysts, and prosecutors. Specifically, police

---

24. Federal Bureau of Investigation. CODIS. http://www.fbi.gov/hq/lab/codis/index1.htm

and sheriffs' department officials need to ask themselves the following questions:

1. What current resources exist within the department and with state, federal, or private entities to assist law enforcement with lab analysis?

2. What federal grants are being offered to assist with lab costs or equipment for the department that can be used in conjunction with lab analysis? Are funding opportunities available from the state government?

3. What are similar cities doing to address DNA demands? Are those initiatives feasible for us? Do local legislators understand the need facing law enforcement with regard to criminal investigations? What are they doing to address the need?

4. What is the current need for DNA analysis? Has this need increased over the last few years? If so, why and how has the need for DNA analysis increased? Project future caseloads based on past trends and current and proposed legislation. Are we likely to experience a surge in DNA cases in the next few years? Consider the increase in DNA caseloads when convicted sex offenders and other felons were mandated to submit DNA samples. How did this change affect the work of the department and investigations on DNA matches to unsolved crimes? Are we prepared for future changes in DNA demands?

5. What is our current training protocol for DNA collection at crime scenes? Who is responsible for the collection and are they receiving appropriate training? Does the chain of custody carry through to the lab?

6. What is our current protocol for prioritizing DNA analysis? Do we have a standard prioritization system in place?

7. Does our department, prosecutor's office or lab use negative evidence witnesses to testify in court? If not, would this be valuable?

8. How does the current crime lab staff interact with detectives? What steps need to be taken to reinforce that relationship to promote better communication, prioritization of evidence analysis, and faster turnaround times? Does the relationship allow the lab staff to remain impartial in reporting their results?

CONCLUSION

Crime labs are a vital part of the criminal justice system. The increase in crime labs and DNA advancements has contributed significantly to solving crimes, and specifically homicides. With this increase has come an overwhelming responsibility to ensure that the science is supported with well-qualified staff, appropriate equipment, and adequate training to manage the caseloads and backlogs. Legislation often results as a good-faith effort to assist law enforcement; however, lawmakers sometimes fail to fully recognize the burden they place on police agency personnel when they mandate new kinds of DNA testing. The laws that require offenders to contribute DNA are indeed a benefit to the criminal justice system, but they are also fostering an overload on the law enforcement community.

More research is needed to understand how DNA affects convictions, clearance rates, staffing, and the criminal justice system overall. DNA is widely accepted as an extremely useful tool in fighting crime, both to keep innocent people from going to jail and to convict the guilty. Nevertheless, the full impact and strains that this technological advancement is having on the criminal justice system need to be explored further.

7

Cold Case Investigations

"Cold case units are essential."

AL CARDARELLI, SENIOR FELLOW AT THE
MCCORMACK GRADUATE SCHOOL OF POLICY
STUDIES, UNIVERSITY OF MASSACHUSETTS, BOSTON

THE RECENT GROWTH OF COLD CASE UNITS CAN BE directly attributed to the improved ability to analyze forensic evidence such as DNA. Though law enforcement agencies have struggled with unsolved cases for years, advances in evidence analysis have greatly improved the ability of cold case units to produce results. Laboratories can now develop DNA profiles from biological evidence that is invisible to the naked eye, whereas a decade ago technicians needed a sample as large as a quarter to complete such tests. Additionally, new testing techniques such as mitochondrial DNA analysis allows laboratories to process degraded evidence that was previously useless forensically.[1]

With these increases in forensic technology capabilities, and decreases in homicide rates in the 1990s freeing up resources in many law enforcement agencies, police started investigating cold cases and some departments formed cold case units. Departments have had significant successes with cold case investigations, solving many homicides and bringing offenders to justice.

---

1. *Using DNA to Solve Cold Cases.* NIJ Special Report, July 2002. National Commission on the Future of DNA Evidence.

Unsolved homicides have bad effects on investigators' productivity; it is more difficult to focus on each new case if there is a large backlog of open cases that still need work. The inability of police departments to close cases can affect police-community relations, as well. When offenders remain free, the level of fear in a community can increase. As a result, police may encounter reluctance and resistance from possible witnesses who fear retaliation from an offender still on the loose. This is especially true for those who live in neighborhoods with high rates of crime and gang-related activity. And, of course, family members and friends of homicide victims continue to experience the additional stress of watching and hoping for an arrest to be made as long as their cases remain unsolved.

As the number of so-called cold cases increases, so, too, does the frustration level among officers. This becomes a vicious cycle: caseloads increase for officers, which reduces the likelihood that new cases will be solved, which can lead to a greater number of homicides because offenders remain free to commit additional homicides or become victims themselves. The need to break this cycle, Professor Al Cardarelli of the University of Massachusetts argues, is one reason why cold case units are essential.

This chapter describes police agencies' experiences with organizing cold case units and their insights on pertinent issues. Departments have taken a number of approaches to organizing and staffing cold case units. These various methods are highlighted so that agencies can determine which model best fits their needs and available resources. The following factors are discussed: staffing, prioritizing cases, opening and pursuing a case, challenges and potential solutions, using the media, and community resources.

COLD CASE UNITS

What is a cold case?

The term "cold case" means different things to different agencies. The definition depends on several factors. In particular, the number of cases and the number of employees available to investigate them will dictate a department's cold case definition. The goal of setting a definition is to include unsolved cases that have grown somewhat old but are not so old that there can be no hope of ever solving them. For instance, some departments consider a case cold if it is unsolved and occurred between 1950 and 2003, because there is still a good chance that witnesses from 1950 may be alive and available for an interview. Other departments have broader definitions that include unsolved cases that are only 1 year old. Still others offer additional clauses. The Las Vegas Metropolitan Police Department, for example, used a tight "working definition" while they organized the unit; officials originally decided *not* to consider a case "cold" if the original investigating officer was still in the department. Once the department gained additional resources for the cold case unit, the definition was amended to include all unsolved cases dating back at least 10 years.

Who works on cold cases?

Although cold case units are relatively new, no one model has emerged as a standard. The consensus among agencies investigating cold cases, however, is that if an agency wishes to investigate cold cases, it should assign individuals full-time to the task. There are numerous examples in which a lone officer, instead of a cold-case team in a separate unit, was assigned cold case tasks, and later was reassigned to new cases because the caseload of active cases was too heavy. As a result, experts suggest that agencies create a specialized cold case unit, assign full-time staff to the unit, organize and prioritize the cold cases. In some agencies, cold case units are a part of the large homicide unit, while in others they are a separate unit.

Typically, the size of the unit is based on a number of factors, including the local homicide rate, the size of the agency, and the number of cold cases on file. There are many approaches to staffing a cold case unit, but nearly all units make use of hybrid staffing that pairs seasoned, sworn officers with experienced and motivated civilian volunteers who have the time to dedicate to the cause of solving cold cases. Civilian review teams analyze cold cases, often relying on solvability factors, and then pass along the most promising cases to active investigators for follow-up. Some of the civilians are retired police officers while others have analytical skills conducive to reviewing case files. The following examples describe arrangements that have proved successful for particular agencies:

Charlotte-Mecklenburg, North Carolina, Police Department
- ESTABLISHED: February 2003

- **OPEN CASES**: 400 cases dating to 1963
- **STAFFING**: Blend of sworn members and civilian volunteers. Sworn members include two homicide detectives, one sergeant, and one FBI agent who is detailed to the Charlotte Safe Streets Task Force.
- **STATUS**: The seven-member civilian review team includes four retired FBI agents, one retired New York Police Department captain, one retired Duke Energy engineer, and a professor from the University of North Carolina–Charlotte. The unit has reviewed 65 cases and has cleared 17.

Las Vegas Metropolitan Police Department

- **ESTABLISHED**: November 2005
- **OPEN CASES**: 550 cases dating from 1943 to 1996, and consistent with agency policy that cases must be more than 10 years old.
- **STAFFING**: A lieutenant and one sworn officer, plus a retired lieutenant and sergeant. Three civilian volunteers assist on a part-time basis.

Chicago Police Department

- **ESTABLISHED**: 1999
- **OPEN CASES**: 4,453 unsolved cases from 1982 through 2002
- **STAFFING**: One lieutenant, two sergeants, 20 detectives, one evidence coordinator, and one administrative aide. Interns from local universities assist the unit with clerical tasks.

Austin, Texas Police Department

- **ESTABLISHED**: 2001
- **OPEN CASES**: 125 cases dating to the 1960s
- **STAFFING**: One sergeant and five detectives are assigned to the unit full-time.

Denver Police Department

- **ESTABLISHED**: 2004
- **OPEN CASES**: A cold case is defined as an open, unsolved case that is at least three years old. The workload currently consists of 30 cases.

- **STAFFING**: Three detectives and a supervisor are dedicated to the cold case unit.

Seattle Police Department
- **ESTABLISHED**: 2001
- **OPEN CASES**: Defined as unsolved homicides going back 30 years.
- **STAFFING**: The unit is composed of a sergeant and two detectives, chosen chiefly for their interviewing skills.
- **STATUS**: Since the unit was established, 34 cases have been reopened, including 25 with DNA samples. All 34 cases have been solved.

As the examples show, the staffing of cold case units differs significantly across agencies. Each agency should consider workload and staff availability when deciding how to staff the unit.

Regarding the people who should staff cold case units, many agencies agree that the following attributes are important:

- **Significant experience in homicide investigations.** One lieutenant went so far as to suggest that it is important to "put your most experienced detectives on the cold case squad."

- **Trial and prosecution experience.** An investigator with this experience typically has better insight into the value of testimony and careful evidence collection.

- **Self-motivation.** People with the desire to work independently fit well into a cold case unit.

- **Compassion.** Investigators must be able to relate to the victim's family and friends.

- **Knowledge of technology and forensics.** The ability to conduct research, to locate information and analyze it effectively, is critical.

- **Communication skills.** Investigators should have effective interviewing and interrogation skills, and should be able to interact with a variety of people.

- **Patience and perseverance.** Those attributes "may be the two most important qualities for working cold cases," stressed one investigator.

Nearly every cold case unit studied has made use of civilian review teams, volunteers, and/or interns. The Las Vegas Metropolitan Police Department hires paid civilian investigative aides to review cases according to solvability criteria. Washington, D.C.'s Metropolitan Police Department solicits assistance from unpaid college interns to review cases. The Charlotte-Mecklenburg Police Department employs unpaid volunteers with law enforcement experience. All volunteers and interns must submit to a background check.

Innovative Approaches

Some departments would like to establish a cold case unit but feel they cannot spare any full-time officers to staff it. The Las Vegas Metropolitan Police Department (LVMPD) may serve as a model for such departments. A lieutenant commands the unit, which also includes two retired investigators. While the investigators had years of experience between them and met all of the qualifications for the job, as retired temporary employees they found it difficult to convince contacts and witnesses to share information. However, LVMPD worked around this impediment by reinstating its Reserve Police Officer Program. The investigators now operate with full law enforcement status, which enhanced their credibility and made tasks such as arrests and affidavits much easier to accomplish. The Reserve Police Officer Program adheres to three primary guidelines. The petitioner must:

- Be retired from the LVMPD
- Be reemployed within 5 years of his or her retirement date
- Continue Police Officer Standards and Training certifications.

The Charlotte-Mecklenburg Police Department also expanded the abilities of its detectives. Using Title 18, Section 566(c) of the U.S. Code, the local law enforcement officers have been granted federal deputy status (i.e., deputized), allowing them a broader jurisdiction. Any federal law enforcement agency can sponsor a state or local law enforcement officer and request the authority to provide the officer with federal deputy status from the U.S. Marshals Service. If an investigation leads detectives to evidence outside of North Carolina, deputized Charlotte-

Mecklenburg detectives would retain the authority to operate. Due to the nature of cold cases, many of the witnesses and suspects have moved away from the area where the crime was committed. This makes travel a necessity for cold case detectives, and makes deputizing extremely useful.

CASE MANAGEMENT

Prioritizing Cold Cases

The unit has been staffed, the policy has been set, and the cold cases have been organized. How should a department decide which case to tackle first? The LVMPD cold case unit created a five-point solvability scale to determine the viability of a particular case. Each of the five levels is differentiated by the information provided in the case report. For instance, cases designated as Level 1—top priority cases—have a file that includes a named suspect, forensic evidence (e.g., DNA, latent fingerprint, firearms ballistics), witness identification of the suspect, and physical evidence that connects the suspect to the victim (e.g., photographs, writing, fibers). Cases that contain all of the above *except* a named suspect are designated as Level 2. Cases that receive lowest priority, Level 5, have only physical evidence as a lead. (See Appendix F for the Las Vegas Metropolitan Police Department's "Cold Case Solvability Criteria" and Appendix G for the Washington, D.C., Metropolitan Police Department's "Homicide Case Review Solvability Chart.")

The Charlotte-Mecklenburg Police Department has developed similar solvability factors for its cold cases. When reviewing files, investigators consider the following questions:

- Does physical evidence exist?

- Is it possible to obtain (from the evidence room) such evidence?

- Was a witness identified?

- Is the suspect living, dead, or incarcerated?

- Is there an opportunity for multiple clearances (i.e., is there a chance this is a serial rapist or killer)?

- Has the case been previously presented to the prosecutors and not accepted for any reason?

Other departments have found that even after prioritizing the cases through the analysis of such criteria, there is still a large number of potential cases from which to choose. So even though a methodical approach was initially followed, publicity generated by their successes led them to concentrate on cases that are brought to their attention through family inquiries and other means.

Opening a Case

The case review process established by the Charlotte-Mecklenburg cold case unit has proved quite successful; the department has received international awards and has been recognized by the Department of Justice as a model for other agencies. Each case is reviewed by the cold case civilian review team and then described at a monthly unit meeting to the entire cold case team, according to the following format:

- Victimology
- Summary of crime
- Medical Examiner's report
- Evidence and/or property collected
- Lab reports
- Witness locations
- Parallel investigations
- Potential suspects
- Recommended follow-up.

At the conclusion of the presentation, unit members discuss the case as a team and assign it a solvability rating between 1 and 5 (1 = high solvability, 5 = low probability of arrest). Detectives previously assigned to the case are also invited to participate in the review, even if they are retired. Often they are able to provide more detailed information than written notes can convey. Once the case is presented, a DNA lab staff member is assigned to the case team, ensuring that any evidence will be processed as quickly as possible. A follow-up report is then written.

The three main benefits of using a civilian review team to open a case are: 1. the summary format model is concise, 2. the legwork completed by the review team allows the detectives more time to actually work the cases, and 3. the summary review can be used to present the case to the district attorney.

Investigators from the Seattle Police Department who attended the PERF conference concurred that it is important to meet with the detectives who originally worked the case to "pick their brains." All departments agreed that meeting with witnesses is another important step that should occur early in the investigation when opening a cold case. Sometimes, investigators have found that relationships change over time and those who were once reluctant to talk are now willing to cooperate. Another technique that has proved fruitful is to track down jailhouse inmates who know, or knew, the suspect. Many times, incarcerated perpetrators confess, or brag, about crimes to their cellmates, who can be persuaded to share this information.

Engaging the Public

People in the community can provide a wealth of information to an investigation. Some community members may have been witnesses to a crime, while others may know—through personal relationships or hearsay—of crimes that have been committed and by whom. Tapping into this knowledge base can help investigators discover relevant leads in cold cases. At the PERF conference on homicide investigations, officials of several departments offered examples of how they publicize their cold cases and engage the public in their own communities.

The Chicago Police Department has learned that it reaches more people, especially the Spanish-speaking population of the city, by taking advantage of media resources. They spotlight cases on Telemundo, the second largest Spanish-language television network in the United States.

The Las Vegas Metropolitan Police Department also recommends using media outlets. The LVMPD publicizes cold cases on both public television stations and the Internet. On television, the department provides details of the case and interviews with family members to generate human interest, and then solicits input from the community.

The Jerri Jones Case

Jerri A. Jones was last seen outside of the Harris Teeter supermarket where she worked in Charlotte, North Carolina, on July 8, 1987. Coworkers recalled seeing her at the store between the end of her shift at 8:30 p.m. and 9:00 p.m. She was reportedly waiting to be picked up by her boyfriend, who was known for running late.

A petite 19-year-old, Jones had been working at Harris Teeter for 2 years and was described by coworkers as an excellent worker and pleasant to be around. She had not planned to remain there much longer, because she was graduating from community college and planning to attend the University of North Carolina the next year.

Based on interviews with friends, family, and acquaintances, investigators concluded in their report that, "There was nothing about her lifestyle that would have made her susceptible to an act of violence."[2] And yet, that is exactly what happened to her. Her body was found 2 days after her disappearance with evidence revealing she had died as a result of a violent assault.

Luckily, investigators had one strong lead: a possible witness to the crime. A woman heard cries for help from the enclosed flatbed area of a white pickup truck the night Jones disappeared. The truck, she reported, had been driving through the Harris Teeter parking lot. Armed with the eyewitness account and a good deal of evidence found at the scene where Ms. Jones' body was found (blood, a cigarette package, a shoe impression, a tire impression, a tie, duct tape, and a rape kit), officers initiated an investigation.

Additionally, Harris Teeter, Inc. offered a $10,000 reward for information leading to the arrest and indictment of the person responsible for Jones' death. The evidence and reward announcement each produced a number of leads, but none was fruitful. A detailed offender

---

[2]. Charlotte-Mecklenburg Police Department investigative case report.

profile provided by the FBI's National Center for the Analysis of Violent Crime (NCAVC) would later prove to be highly accurate, but at the time did not help the investigative team to pinpoint the perpetrator either.

Fast-forward 17 years: A civilian review team at the Charlotte-Mecklenburg Police Department presented its draft report to the cold case unit on September 3, 2004. The 99-page report outlined the original investigation into the homicide of Ms. Jones. Details included the summary of the crime, the medical examiner's report, a crime scene summary report, a list of property and evidence recovered, the NCAVC profile, missing person investigation results, a canvass report, a list of witnesses, handwritten notes, a list of potential suspects, and, finally, recommended follow-up.

Investigators decided to test the rape kit for the existence of DNA. The kits were sent to the department's forensic lab and within 10 days the results came back positive for DNA. In addition, the results matched preexisting samples belonging to Terry Alvin Hyatt, who was serving time on North Carolina's death row for two first-degree homicide convictions; both involved female victims.

Although Hyatt was on death row, he was also in the midst of an appeal process. Prosecutors presented their case to his attorneys and he agreed to plead to first degree homicide with a life-without-parole sentence, avoiding another death penalty conviction.

Harris Teeter stayed true to its word and donated the $10,000 reward to the Charlotte-Mecklenburg Police Department's forensic lab. ∎

The LVMPD and an increasing number of other departments use the Internet to publicize cases investigations. An e-mail address and local tip line are posted on the site. The vast majority of responses have been received through e-mail and run the gamut from inquiries and stories to serious tips. Tips are submitted by other law enforcement agency personnel, retired law enforcement personnel, friends and neighbors of victims, and of course family members. Detectives welcome the responses. Not only do the tips help them to prioritize cases, but they have also helped to reduce the number of open cases.

Other Resources

Those with experience in cold case investigations have found a number of allies in the community, in part because their agencies have worked diligently to implement programs consistent with community policing. The following steps are recommended to improve community relationships and enhance the department's ability to solve cold cases:

- Reach out to victim assistance and advocacy organizations.

- Reconnect with families of victims.

- Advertise for volunteers (media coverage might inspire them to offer assistance without prompting).

- Work with the prosecutor's office. Apprise them of the cold case unit's development and progress.

- Nurture or develop a relationship with the U.S. Marshals Service liaison, who can assist with apprehending suspects in other states.

The National Center for Missing & Exploited Children's (NCMEC) Project ALERT (America's Law Enforcement Retiree Team) program is also available to assist cold case units or law enforcement agencies with cold cases involving victims younger than 21 years old.

The Project ALERT program uses retired law enforcement investigators who have been specially selected, trained, and certified. These Project ALERT representatives act as consultants and are deployed to law enforcement agencies across the nation—*free of charge*—to assist investigators. As former criminal investigators, they bring a wealth of investigative experience, skills, and abilities to assist on these cases.

The Project ALERT representatives also bring access to all of NCMEC's other resources, including help with case management and crime analysis, specialized training, and poster distribution. NCMEC also has partnerships with experts in conducting searches for missing persons (such as NecroSearch, a nonprofit organization that specializes in the search for clandestine gravesites, and specialized canine groups) as well as professional forensic laboratories to assist with the evidentiary aspects of cold cases.

Crime analysts are another resource that can assist cold case investigations. Database searches, link-analysis charts, timelines, and maps detailing the incident and the events, witnesses and locations associated with it, are tools that a crime analyst has expertise in using effectively. Analysts often maintain listservs as well, which are useful for communicating with and keeping abreast of what is happening in other jurisdictions.

Evidence

Investigators must possess patience, because cold cases are not without their challenges. Experienced cold case investigators often cite the following challenges concerning physical evidence:

- **Collection and Analysis.** In the past, investigators may not have collected the evidence needed to identify a suspect, because many of the tests used today did not exist years ago. Also, traditional methods of forensic analysis may have used all of the evidence in the original processing, so little or none may be left to analyze using the new technologies.
- **Deterioration.** Evidence may have deteriorated because of the passage of time and improper packaging and/or storage.
- **Missing Evidence.** It is not uncommon for evidence to be misplaced or lost during office moves, file purging, misplacement, and other accidents.

Consulting the Coroner's Office[3]

Detective Kevin Manning of the Las Vegas Metropolitan Police Department's (LVMPD) Cold Case Unit recently discovered this resource while investigating a case. In April 2006, a man contacted the department to inquire about the homicide of a former high school classmate that occurred in 1981. Manning pulled the file and discovered that a suspect had been arrested, but the case was dismissed. (The reason for dismissal was not detailed in the file.) He noticed that a sexual assault also occurred, so he visited the evidence vault to collect the rape kit.

Unfortunately, he found no record of the evidence. He decided to consult the file once more, and that is when he read that vaginal swabs had been collected during the autopsy. At this point, he contacted the coroner's office and discovered it still had the swabs in its possession. Detective Manning was able to obtain this evidence and submit it to the LVMPD DNA lab. He is now waiting for the results. In the meantime, the suspect was served an affidavit in Iowa, where he now resides.

Evidence stored at the coroner's office was helpful again when Detective Manning investigated a homicide that occurred in 1983. A teenage girl, home for Christmas break, went for a jog and never returned. Her body was found, with evidence indicating she had been raped and stabbed. In 1988, another woman was attacked in the same manner—but after the rape she was able to escape and identify her assailant, who was subsequently arrested. Investigators believed that the same man committed the 1983 homicide, but when Manning went to the evidence room to obtain the sexual assault kit, he found that the kit had been purged. Once again, he contacted the coroner's office, which had this case on file. Testing is now under way; the suspect remains in jail for the 1988 sexual assault conviction. ∎

---

3. Based on interviews in 2006 with Detective Manning of the Las Vegas Metropolitan Police Department.

If the evidence is lost, misplaced, or has deteriorated, one possible solution is to contact the coroner's office. Agencies have discovered that the coroner's office has often collected and stored its own evidence samples and are happy to assist with the investigation of a cold case.

CONSIDERATIONS FOR LAW ENFORCEMENT AGENCIES

Although best practices for creating and maintaining a cold case unit have not been documented and published, numerous models are available to guide agencies. To create a cold case unit, the following factors should be considered:

- How many investigators can be spared from the existing homicide unit or other investigative units?
- Does the department have a recruitment program for civilian volunteers?
- Are there retired investigators who would be interested in joining the unit?
- What is the jurisdiction's current homicide rate?
- How many unsolved cases are in the department's files?

Taking stock of resources will help departments determine their next steps. If resources from the current homicide investigations team cannot be spared, departments may consider using the LVMPD Cold Case Unit as a model for staffing entirely with full-time retired personnel and civilian volunteers. Other models are available to fit the diverse needs of law enforcement agencies across the country.

The most important factor of all is to consider how solving cold cases will benefit the department and the community it serves. According to Professor Cardarelli, the establishment of a cold case unit will accomplish the following:

- Solve homicides and lead to the prosecution of offenders
- Improve the department's clearance rate

- Improve officer productivity
- Increase public confidence in law enforcement.

Furthermore, cold case units' personnel report a high level of personal satisfaction when they close a case. Unsolved homicides create deep feelings of loss and anger in the survivors of homicide victims, and by solving these homicides investigators can ease the suffering of survivors. Even when a case cannot be solved, the efforts of the investigator are often greatly appreciated by the friends and family of the victim. Establishing a cold case unit and rotating officers through it, therefore, could be a welcome and rewarding experience for police employees.

CONCLUSION

The rewards associated with the development of a cold case unit are significant. Case clearance rates increase, guilty parties are brought to justice, innocent parties are exonerated, victims' survivors get a measure of relief, and investigators benefit from the personal satisfaction associated with solving cold cases. Police departments have achieved these benefits using a variety of organizational and staffing arrangements, depending on their resources and caseloads. Regardless of how a cold case unit is organized, the resounding message from those with experience is that as long as it is staffed with passionate, patient, and experienced investigators, it will be a successful endeavor.

About the Authors

JAMES M. CRONIN

James M. Cronin is a Research Associate for PERF's Center on Force and Accountability. Since starting work at PERF in 2005, Mr. Cronin has become a member of the U.S. Department of Justice's Less Lethal Working Group and has been actively involved in research concerning the use of conducted energy devices by law enforcement agencies.

Prior to joining PERF, Cronin worked as a researcher for the Maryland Statistical Analysis Center, the Bureau of Governmental Research (HIDTA-High Intensity Drug Trafficking Areas), the Washington, D.C., Sentencing Commission, and the D.C. Criminal Justice Coordinating Council. He has conducted research on juvenile delinquency prevention, homicide clearance rates, and the rehabilitation of offenders. He also assisted in establishing sentencing guidelines for the District of Columbia.

Mr. Cronin received his master of arts degree in Criminology and Criminal Justice in 1994 from the University of Maryland.

GERARD R. MURPHY

Gerard Murphy serves as PERF's Director of Homeland Security and Development and oversees all PERF homeland security-related projects. In this capacity he manages a variety of research, management, and technical assistance projects focusing on law enforcement and homeland security. In addition, he oversees the development of ideas for new projects for PERF.

In his 12 years at PERF, Mr. Murphy has directed a variety of research and technical assistance projects and has written or cowritten numerous PERF publications. One of his most recent publications is *Managing a Multijurisdictional Case: Identifying the Lessons Learned from the Sniper Investigation*. Mr. Murphy also spent 12 years with the Baltimore County

Police Department, holding the positions of Assistant to the Chief and Director of Planning and Research.

Mr. Murphy holds a master's degree in policy sciences, has completed extensive work towards his doctorate in policy sciences, and is a graduate of the Federal Executive Institute.

LISA L. SPAHR

Lisa Spahr was an Associate for PERF's Center on Force and Accountability. She has more than 12 years of experience in research and development in law enforcement, corrections and law, and psychiatry. At PERF, Ms. Spahr managed multiple research projects, including the 2006 *Critical Issues in Policing Series,* patrol response to suicide bombing threats, redesigning an officer discipline system, and less-lethal weapons' impact on injuries and liabilities.

Prior to joining PERF, Ms. Spahr served as a Project Manager for the University of Pittsburgh, Law and Psychiatry Research Department. Ms. Spahr has also served as an adjunct faculty member, instructing in both law enforcement and psychology coursework, and has managed a community corrections facility in Philadelphia.

Ms. Spahr received her bachelor of arts degree in psychology from Temple University, and a master of science degree in investigative psychology from the University of Liverpool, England.

JESSICA I. TOLIVER

Jessica Ingenito Toliver joined PERF as a Research Associate in April 2005. Since arriving at PERF, she has been a contributing author for the *Police Management of Mass Demonstration* publication and the *Improving the Response to Elder Abuse* training curriculum for law enforcement agencies. Currently, she manages the "Meth 360" program, a methamphetamine demand reduction strategy created by the Partnership for a Drug-Free America, sponsored by the COPS Office.

Prior to joining PERF, she served as a Policy Analyst in the Homeland Security and Technology Division at the National Governors Association. Ms. Toliver also completed a fellowship for Governor Jennifer M. Granholm's office in 2003, in which she conducted a cost-benefit analysis of the Michigan State Police's DNA forensic labs.

Ms. Toliver received her bachelor's degree in political science and journalism from the University of Richmond and her master's degree in public policy from the Gerald R. Ford School of Public Policy at the University of Michigan.

RICHARD E. WEGER

Richard Weger came to PERF from the San Jose Police Department on a 6-month fellowship in the Center on Force and Accountability.

Lieutenant Weger has served as a member of the San Jose, California, Police Department (SJPD) since 1990. He has worked Patrol, Youth Services, and Gang Investigations. He left SJPD when he was hired as a Special Agent with the FBI. Two years later, Mr. Weger returned home to the SJPD where he worked as a Field Training Officer and as a high-tech investigator. He also served as aide to Chief of Police Robert L. Davis. He continues to teach police academy recruits in a variety of subjects.

Mr. Weger obtained his bachelor's degree in the administration of justice from San Jose State University in 1993.

About the COPS Office

THE OFFICE OF COMMUNITY ORIENTED POLICING SERVICES (the COPS Office) was created in 1994 and has the unique mission of directly serving the needs of state and local law enforcement. The COPS Office has been the driving force in advancing the concept of community policing and is responsible for one of the greatest infusions of resources into state, local, and tribal law enforcement in our nation's history.

Since 1994, the COPS Office has invested more than $11.4 billion to add community policing officers to the nation's streets, enhance crime fighting technology, support crime prevention initiatives, and provide training and technical assistance to help advance community policing. COPS Office funding has furthered the advancement of community policing through community policing innovation conferences, the development of best practices, pilot community policing programs, and applied research and evaluation initiatives. The COPS Office has also positioned itself to respond directly to emerging law enforcement needs. Examples include working in partnership with departments to enhance police integrity, promoting safe schools, combating the methamphetamine drug problem, and supporting homeland security efforts.

Through its grant programs, the COPS Office assists and encourages local, state, and tribal law enforcement agencies in enhancing their homeland security efforts using proven community policing strategies. Traditional COPS Office programs such as the Universal Hiring Program (UHP) give priority consideration to those applicants that demonstrate a use of funds related to terrorism preparedness or response through community policing. The COPS in Schools (CIS) program has a mandatory training component that includes topics on terrorism prevention, emergency response, and the critical role schools can play in community response. Finally, the COPS Office has implemented grant programs intended to develop interoperable voice and data communications networks among emergency response agencies that will assist in addressing local homeland security demands.

The COPS Office has made substantial investments in law enforcement training. The COPS Office created a national network of Regional Community Policing Institutes (RCPI) that are available to state and local law enforcement, elected officials, and community leaders for training opportunities on a wide range of community policing topics. Recently, the RCPIs have focused their efforts on developing and delivering homeland security training. In addition, the COPS Office has made a major investment in applied research, which makes possible the growing body of substantive knowledge covering all aspects of community policing.

These substantial investments have produced a significant community policing infrastructure across the country as evidenced by the fact that at the present time, approximately 86 percent of the nation's population is served by law enforcement agencies practicing community policing. The COPS Office continues to respond proactively by providing critical resources, training, and technical assistance to help state, local, and tribal law enforcement implement innovative and effective community policing strategies.

About PERF

THE POLICE EXECUTIVE RESEARCH FORUM (PERF) IS A NATIONAL organization of progressive law enforcement chief executives from city, county and state agencies who collectively serve more than half of the country's population. Established in 1976 by 10 prominent police chiefs, PERF has evolved into one of the leading police think tanks. With membership from many of the larger police departments in the country and around the globe, PERF has pioneered studies in such fields as community and problem-oriented policing, racially biased policing, multijurisdictional investigations, domestic violence, law enforcement response to people with mental illnesses, homeland security, management concerns, use of force, and crime-reduction approaches.

PERF's success is built on the active involvement of its members: police chiefs, superintendents, sheriffs, and other law enforcement leaders. The organization also has various types of membership that allow the organization to benefit from the diverse views of criminal justice researchers, law enforcement of all ranks, and others committed to advancing policing services to all communities. As a nonprofit organization, PERF is committed to the application of research in policing and to promoting innovation that will enhance the quality of life in our communities. PERF's objective is to improve the delivery of police services and the effectiveness of crime control through the exercise of strong national leadership, the public debate of criminal justice issues, the development of a body of research about policing, and the provision of vital management services to all police agencies.

In addition to its cutting-edge research and management and technical assistance programs, PERF continues to work toward increased professionalism and excellence in the field through its training, leadership, and publications programs. For example, PERF sponsors the Senior Management Institute for Police (SMIP), conducts searches for communities seeking police chief executives, and publishes some of the leading literature in the law enforcement field that addresses the difficult issues that challenge today's police leaders. PERF publications are used for training and promotion exams and to inform police professionals about innovative approaches to community problems. The hallmark of the publications program is translating the latest research and thinking about a topic into police practices that can be tailored to the unique needs of a jurisdiction.

APPENDIX A

Conference Participants

Police Executive Research Forum
Homicide Investigations Conference
May 25–26, 2006

Charlie Adams
Sergeant
Minneapolis Police Department
350 S. 5th St., Room 130
Minneapolis, MN 55415
Charlie.Adams@ci.minneapolis.mn.us
612.673.2941

Michael Anzallo
Commander
Metropolitan (D.C.) Police
 Department
300 Indiana Avenue, NW
Washington, DC 20001
michael.anzallo@dc.gov
202.727.7787

Andres Arostegui
Detective
Miami Police Department
400 NW Second Avenue
Miami, FL 33128
andres.arostegui@miami-police.org
305.579.6530

Patricia Bailey
Assistant District Attorney
New York County District Attorney's
 Office
1 Hogan Place
New York, NY 10013
baileyp@dany.nyc.gov
212.335.4362

Judith Beres
Editor
The COPS Office
1100 Vermont Avenue, NW
Washington, DC 20530
judith.beres@usdoj.gov
202.353.4010

Karl Bickel
Senior Policy Analyst
The COPS Office
1100 Vermont Avenue, NW
Washington, DC 20530
Karl.Bickel@usdoj.gov
202.514.5914

John Buhrmaster
Lieutenant
Miami Police Department
400 NW Second Avenue
Miami, FL 33128
john.buhrmaster@miami-police.org
305.579.6530

Pam Cammarata
Deputy Director
COPS Office
1100 Vermont Ave., NW, 10th Floor
Washington, DC 20530
Pam.Cammarata@usdoj.gov
202.514.9193

Al Cardarelli
Senior Fellow
McCormack Graduate School of Policy Studies, University of Massachusetts Boston
100 Morrissey Boulevard
Boston, MA 02125
albert.cardarelli@verizon.net
617.524.2588

Alexander Casas
Captain
Miami Dade Police Department
9105 NW 25 Street, Suite 2088
Doral, FL 33172-1500
acasas@mdpd.com
305.471.2400

Jason Cheney
Research Assistant
PERF
1120 Connecticut Ave. NW, Suite 930
Washington, DC 20036
jcheney@policeforum.org
202.454.8331

Jung–Won Choi
Assistant General Counsel
FBI
jung.choi@ic.fbi.gov
202.324.9625

Daniel Coleman
Deputy Superintendent
Boston Police Department
One Schroeder Plaza
Boston, MA 02120
Colemand.bpd@ci.boston.ma.us
617.343.4470

James Cronin
Research Associate
PERF
1120 Connecticut Ave. NW, Suite 930
Washington, DC 20036
jcronin@policeforum.org
202.454.8319

Milton Dale Brown
Captain
Houston Police Department
1200 Travis, 6th Floor
Houston, TX 77002
Milton.Brown@cityofhouston.net
713.308.3989

Dr. Heather Davies
Associate
Strategic Analysis, Inc.
One Virginia Square, 3601 Wilson Blvd., Suite 500
Arlington, VA 22201
hdavies@sainc.com
703.276.2229

John Davison
Detective
Dallas Police Department
1400 S. Lamar St.
Dallas, TX 75215
john.davison@dpd.dallascityhall.com
214.671.3687

Jim Dillon
Captain
Las Vegas Metropolitan Police
  Department
400 Stewart Avenue
Las Vegas, NV 89101
j2239d@lvmpd.com
702.229.3528

James Doyle
Director
Center for Modern Forensic Practice,
  John Jay College of Criminal Justice
20 Park Plaza, Suite 1405
Boston, MA 02116
james@truewitness.us
617.338.5566

Rod Drew
Detective Superintendent
New Zealand Police
37 Observatory Circle
Washington D.C. 20008
Rod.drew@police.govt.nz

Josh Ederheimer
Director, Center on Force and
  Accountability
PERF
1120 Connecticut Ave. NW, Suite 930
Washington, DC 20036
jederheimer@policeforum.org
202.454.8317

Anthony Ell
Major
Kansas City Police Department
1125 Locust St.
Kansas City, MO 64106
aell@kcpd.org
816.234.5211

Michael J. Farrell
Deputy Commissioner
NYPD
One Police Plaza, Room 1400
New York, NY 10038
mfarrell@nypd.org
646.610.8534

Larry Ford
Assistant Director
ATF
650 Massachusetts Avenue, NW.
Washington, DC 20226
Allison.cibroski@atf.gov
202.927.8500

J. R. Francomano
Assistant State's Attorney
Baltimore County State's Attorney's
  Office
401 Bosley Ave., Room 511
Towson, MD 21204
jfrancomano@co.ba.md.us
410.887.6630

Brad Garrett
Special Agent
FBI
601 4th Street, N.W.
Washington, DC 20535
brad.garrett@earthlink.net
202.278.2373

Robert Giannelli
Deputy Chief
NYPD
One Police Plaza, Room 1312
New York, NY 10038
robert.giannelli@nypd.org
646.610.5430

Tag Gleason
Captain
Seattle Police Department
610 5th Ave., P.O. Box 34986
Seattle, WA 98124
GleasonT@Seattle.Gov
206.684.5531

Rudy Gonzalez
Lieutenant
Miami Dade Police Department
9105 NW 25 Street, Suite 2088
Doral, FL 33172-1500
r_gonzalez01@mdpd.com
305.471.2400

Peter Grippi
Sergeant
Baltimore County Police Department
700 East Joppa Road
Towson, MD 21286-5501
pgrippi@co.ba.md.us
410.887.3943

Mark Hanf
Detective
Seattle Police Department
610 5th Ave., PO Box 34986
Seattle, WA 98124
HanfM@Seattle.Gov
206.684.8034

Shelia Hargis
Crime Analysis Supervisor
Austin Police Department
P.O. Box 689001
Austin, TX 78768-9001
Shelia.Hargis@ci.austin.tx.us
512.974.5951

Ray Harp
Director, Project ALERT
National Center for Missing and
 Exploited Children
699 Prince Street
Alexandria, VA 22314
RHarp@NCMEC.ORG
703.837.6219

Robert Harrington
Lt. Detective
Boston Police Department
One Schroeder Plaza
Boston, MA 02120
HarringtonR.bpd@ci.boston.ma.us
617.343.4470

Alan Harris
**Senior Assistant Hennepin County
 Attorney**
Hennepin County Attorney's Office
C-2100 Hennepin County
 Government Center
Minneapolis, MN 55487
alan.harris@co.hennepin.mn.us
612.348.2120

Nannette Hegerty
Chief
Milwaukee Police Department
749 W. State Street
Milwaukee, WI 53233
nheger@milwaukee.gov
414.935.7200

Maggie Heisler
Senior Social Science Analyst
National Institute of Justice
810 7th Street, NW
Washington, DC 20531
Maggie.Heisler@usdoj.gov
202.616.3452

Charles Hoffman
First Sergeant
Prince William County Police
 Department
15948 Donald Curtis Drive
Woodbridge, VA 22191
choffman@pwcgov.org
703.792.6410

Mitch Hollis
Sergeant
Montgomery County Police
 Department
2350 Research Blvd.
Rockville, MD 20850
mitchell.hollis@montgomerycounty
 md.gov
240.773.5070

Rick Jackson
Detective
LAPD
150 North Los Angeles St., Room 321
Los Angeles, CA 90012
rjackson187@msn.com
213.847.0970

Dennis Keane
Lieutenant
Chicago Police Department
3510 South Michigan Avenue
Chicago, IL 60653
Dennis.Keane@chicagopolice.org
312.747.8272

Tim Keel
Major Case Specialist
FBI-NCAVC, Behavioral Analysis Unit
FBI Academy
Quantico, VA 22135
tgkeel@fbiacademy.edu
703.632.4345

Alan Knox
Crime Analyst
Minneapolis Police Department
350 S. 5th St., Room 130
Minneapolis, MN 55415
Alan.Knox@ci.minneapolis.mn.us
612.673.2941

Irvin Litofsky
Director, Forensic Services Section
Baltimore County Police Department
700 East Joppa Road
Towson, MD 21286-5501
ilitofsky@co.ba.md.us
410.887.2290

Maria Maher
Chief of Detective Division
Chicago Police Department
3510 South Michigan Avenue
Chicago, IL 60653
Maria.Maher@chicagopolice.org
312.745.6016

Lisa Mangum
Sergeant
Charlotte-Mecklenburg Police
 Department
601 East Trade Street
Charlotte, NC 28202
mmangum@cmpd.org
704.336.2294

Walter Martin
Assistant Chief
Detroit Police Department
1300 Beaubien, Suite, 318
Detroit MI, 48226
martinw476@dpdhq.ci.detroit.mi.us
313.596.6116

Paul Masterson
Detective
Prince William County Police
  Department
15948 Donald Curtis Drive
Woodbridge, VA 22191
pmasterson@pwcgov.org
703.792.7279

Sheri Mecklenburg
Director of Illinois Pilot Program on
  Eyewitness Identification/General
  Counsel to Superintendent,
  Chicago Police Department
Chicago Police Department
3510 South Michigan Avenue
Chicago, IL 60653
sheri.mecklenburg@chicagopolice.org
312.745.6115

Lois Mock
Senior Social Science Analyst
National Institute of Justice
810 7th Street, NW
Washington, DC 20531
Lois.Mock@usdoj.gov
202.307.0693

Michel Moore
Deputy Chief
LAPD
11121 North Sepulveda Blvd.
Mission Hills, CA 91345
mooremi@lapd.lacity.org
818.838.9465

C. Verro Morris
Captain
Metropolitan (DC) Police
  Department
3244 Pennsylvania Ave., SE
Washington, DC 20032
charles.morris@dc.gov
202.645.6363

Jerry Murphy
Director, Homeland Security and
  Development
PERF
1120 Connecticut Ave., NW, Suite 930
Washington, DC 20036
gmurphy@policeforum.org
202.454.8314

Dana Murphy
Director of Communications
PERF
1120 Connecticut Ave., NW, Suite 930
Washington, DC 20036
dmurphy@policeforum.org
202.454.8332

Rebecca Neuburger
Membership Administrator
PERF
1120 Connecticut Ave., NW, Suite 930
Washington, DC 20036
rneuburger@policeforum.org
202.454.8300

Dr. Mallory O'Brien
Project Director
Milwaukee Homicide Review
  Commission, Harvard Injury
  Control Research Center
2501 E. Menlo Boulevard
Milwaukee, WI 53211
mobrien@hsph.harvard.edu
414.935.7614

Brian O'Keefe
Deputy Chief
Milwaukee Police Department
749 W. State Street
Milwaukee, WI 53233
bokeef@milwaukee.gov
414.935.7300

Cynthia Pappas
Senior Social Science Analyst
The COPS Office
1100 Vermont Ave., NW
Washington, DC 20530
Cynthia.pappas@usdoj.gov
202.514.8252

Robert Parker
Sergeant
Metropolitan (DC) Police
  Department
3244 Pennsylvania Ave., SE
Washington DC 20032
robert.parker@dc.gov
202.645.6363

Alison Pastor
Intern
PERF
1120 Connecticut Ave., NW, Suite 930
Washington, DC 20036
apastor@policeforum.org
202.454.8315

Anthony Patterson
Detective
Metropolitan (DC) Police
  Department
3244 Pennsylvania Ave., SE
Washington DC 20032
Anthony.Patterson@dc.gov
202.645.6363

Carl Peed
Director
COPS Office
1100 Vermont Avenue, NW
Washington, DC 20530
carl.peed@usdoj.gov
202.616.2888

Jonathyn Priest
Lieutenant
Denver Police Department
1331 Cherokee St.
Denver, CO 80204
Jonathyn.Priest@ci.denver.co.us
720.913.6697

Pete Ramirez
Sergeant
San Jose Police Department
201 West Mission St.
San Jose, CA 95110
pete.ramirez@sanjoseca.gov
408.277.5283

Corey Ray
Public Liaison Specialist
The COPS Office
1100 Vermont Avenue, NW
Washington, DC 20530
corey.ray@usdoj.gov
202.514.5328

Winnie Reed
Acting Chief, Crime Control and
  Prevention Division
National Institute of Justice
810 7th Street, NW
Washington, DC 20531
Winnie.Reed@usdoj.gov
202.307.2952

Alfredo Saldana
Deputy Chief
Dallas Police Department
1400 S. Lamar St.
Dallas, TX 75215
alfredo.saldana@dpd.dallascityhall.com
214.671.3581

Amy Schapiro
Senior Social Science Analyst
The COPS Office
1100 Vermont Avenue, NW, 10th Floor
Washington, DC 20530
amy.schapiro@usdoj.gov
202.514.8721

Glenn Schmitt
Director
National Institute of Justice
810 7th Street, NW
Washington, DC 20531
Glenn.Schmitt@usdoj.gov
202.307.2942

John Sheridan
Sergeant
Montgomery County Police Department
2350 Research Blvd.
Rockville, MD 20850
john.sheridan@montgomerycountymd.gov
240.773.5070

Murray Smith
Lieutenant
Houston Police Department
1200 Travis, 6th Floor
Houston, TX 77002
Murray.Smith@cityofhouston.net
713.308.3922

Lisa Spahr
Research Associate
PERF
1120 Connecticut Ave., NW, Suite 930
Washington, DC 20036
lspahr@policeforum.org
202.454.8343

Richard Stanek
Captain
Minneapolis Police Department
350 S. 5th St., Room 130
Minneapolis, MN 55415
Richard.Stanek@ci.minneapolis.mn.us
612.673.2218

Melissa Staples
Lieutenant
Chicago Police Department
3315 W. Ogden
Chicago, IL 60623
melissa.staples@chicagopolice.org
312.747.7220

Nancy Steblay
Professor
Augsburg College
Campus Box 32, 2211 Riverside Avenue
Minneapolis MN 55454
steblay@augsburg.edu
612.330.1201

Stephanie Stoiloff
Senior Police Bureau Commander
Miami Dade Police Department
9105 NW 25 Street, Suite 2154
Doral, FL 33172-1500
sstoiloff@mdpd.com
305.471.2050

Mike Thaler
Executive Assistant Chief
Houston Police Department
1200 Travis, 6th Floor
Houston, TX 77002
mike.thaler@cityofhouston.net
713.308.1572

Jessica Toliver
Research Associate
PERF
1120 Connecticut Ave., NW, Suite 930
Washington, DC 20036
jtoliver@policeforum.org
202.454.8344

Jim Trainum
Detective
Metropolitan (DC) Police
 Department/OSD
300 Indiana Avenue, NW
Washington, DC 20001
james.trainum@dc.gov
202.727.5037

Louis Vega
Assistant Chief
Miami Police Department
400 NW Second Avenue
Miami, FL 33128
louis.vega@miami-police.org
305.579.6521

Ron Waldrop
Assistant Chief
Dallas Police Department
1400 S. Lamar St.
Dallas, TX 75215
ronald.waldrop@dpd.dallascityhall.com
214.671.3912

John Wallace
Detective
Fairfax County Police Department
4100 Chain Bridge Road
Fairfax, VA 22030
John.Wallace@fairfaxcounty.gov
703.246.7597

Rick Weger
Sergeant/PERF Fellow
San Jose Police Department/PERF
1120 Connecticut Ave. NW, Suite 930
Washington, DC 20036
rweger@policeforum.org
202.454.8304

Charles Wellford
Professor
University of Maryland
2220 Le Frak Hall
College Park, MD 20742
cwellford@crim.umd.edu
301.405.4701

Chuck Wexler
Executive Director
PERF
1120 Connecticut Ave., NW, Suite 930
Washington, DC 20036
cwexler@policeforum.org
202.466.7820

Nina Wright
Deputy Chief
Charlotte-Mecklenburg Police
 Department
601 East Trade Street
Charlotte, NC 28202
nwright@cmpd.org
704.336.2345

Jim Young
Sergeant
Las Vegas Metropolitan Police
 Department
400 Stewart Avenue
Las Vegas, NV 89101
j3166y@lvmpd.com
702.812.0117

Rick Zimmerman
Sergeant
Minneapolis Police Department
350 S. 5th St., Room 130
Minneapolis, MN 55415
Richard.Zimmerman@ci.minneapolis.mn.us
612.673.2941

Paul Zinkann III
Captain
Charlotte-Mecklenburg Police Department
601 East Trade Street
Charlotte, NC 28202
pzinkann1@cmpd.org
704.336.6873

APPENDIX B

External Resources and Strategies for Homicide Units

VIOLENT CRIMINAL APPREHENSION PROGRAM (ViCAP)

ViCAP is a national database on crimes of violence. ViCAP's mission is to facilitate cooperation, communication, and coordination between law enforcement agencies and provide support in their efforts to investigate, identify, track, apprehend, and prosecute violent serial offenders. The FBI provides the software to state and local law enforcement agencies, allowing them to connect to the ViCAP database. ViCAP detects common characteristics of the homicide and similar patterns of modus operandi, allowing ViCAP personnel to pinpoint those crimes that potentially have been committed by the same offender. When patterns are found, involved law enforcement agencies are notified of the results so they may pursue the information for lead value.

Detective Jim Trainum of the Washington, D.C. Metropolitan Police Department has used ViCAP extensively and speaks favorably of the program. He did, however, point out that collecting and inputting data is time consuming. Detective Trainum uses funding from backlog reduction grants and college interns to input ViCAP data. ViCAP is currently being used to investigate serial sexual assaults and homicides in Washington D.C.*

---

*Trainum, J. *Violent Criminal Apprehension Team and the Washington, D.C., Metropolitan Police Department*. Detective Trainum's remarks at the Police Executive Research Forum Homicide Conference, Washington, D.C., May 2006.

PROJECT SAFE NEIGHBORHOODS (PSN)

PSN is a nationwide program to reduce gun violence in America by networking existing local programs and providing these programs with additional resources. PSN funding, which is provided by the National Institute of Justice, is being used to hire new federal and state prosecutors, support investigators, provide training, distribute gun lock safety kits, deter juvenile gun crime, and develop and promote community outreach efforts as well as to support other gun violence reduction strategies.

VIOLENT CRIME IMPACT TEAM (VCIT)

The Bureau of Alcohol, Tobacco, Firearms and Explosives created VCITs in 15 U.S. communities. VCIT works in conjunction with Project Safe Neighborhoods, building on the success of PSN, but adding additional resources to the targeted cities. This initiative has placed teams of federal, state, and local law enforcement officers and prosecutors in each selected city. The goal of the program is to identify and arrest the most violent offenders in each city. The VCIT initiative takes a six-point approach to reducing violent crime:

1. Use technology and human intelligence to identify geographic areas within the targeted cities with violent firearms crime.

2. Identify and target the worst violent offenders, the criminal organizations that support them, and determine how many are career criminals.

3. Use criminal investigations as well as investigative tools and resources to disrupt and dismantle criminal activity being perpetrated by the targeted individuals and organizations.

4. Arrest and prosecute the targeted individuals and their associates in the federal or state jurisdiction that lends itself to the most appropriate penalty.

5. Work with community leaders to cultivate solid and sustained commitment between the community's residents and law enforcement.

6. Evaluate results on a monthly basis to assess VCIT progress toward achieving the initiative's goals.

APPENDIX C

Guidelines for Preparing and Conducting Photo and Live Lineup Identification Procedures

State of New Jersey
DEPARTMENT OF LAW AND PUBLIC SAFETY

DONALD T. DIFRANCESCO *Acting Governor*	OFFICE OF THE ATTORNEY GENERAL PO Box 080 TRENTON, NJ 08625-008 (609) 292-4925	**JOHN J. FARMER, JR.** *Attorney General*

April 18, 2001

TO: ALL COUNTY PROSECUTORS

COL. CARSON J. DUNBAR, JR., SUPERINTENDENT, NJSP

ALL POLICE CHIEFS

ALL LAW ENFORCEMENT CHIEF EXECUTIVES

Re: Attorney General Guidelines for Preparing and Conducting Photo and Live Lineup Identification Procedures

It is axiomatic that eyewitness identification evidence is often crucial in identifying perpetrators and exonerating the innocent. However, recent cases, in which DNA evidence has been utilized to exonerate individuals convicted almost exclusively on the basis of eyewitness identifications, demonstrate that this evidence is not fool-proof. In one 1998 study of DNA exoneration cases, ninety percent of the cases analyzed involved one or more mistaken eyewitness identifications.[1]

The attached *Attorney General Guidelines for Preparing and Conducting Photo and Live Lineup Identification Procedures,* which incorporate more than 20 years of scientific research on memory and interview techniques, will improve the eyewitness identification process in New Jersey to ensure that the criminal justice system will fairly and effectively elicit accurate and reliable eyewitness evidence. These Guidelines apply to both adult and juvenile cases. With these Guidelines, New Jersey will become the first state in the Nation to officially adopt the recommendations issued by the United States Department of Justice in its *Eyewitness Evidence Guidelines.*

Components of these Guidelines are already being utilized by many of our law enforcement officers, such as instructing witnesses prior to lineups or photo identifications that a perpetrator may not be among those in a lineup or photo spread and, therefore, the witness should not feel compelled to make an identification. Two procedural recommendations contained in these Guidelines are particularly significant and will represent the primary area of change for most law enforcement agencies. The first advises agencies to utilize, whenever practical, someone other than the primary investigator assigned to a case to conduct both photo and live lineup identifications. The individual conducting the photo or live lineup identification should not know the identity of the actual suspect. This provision of the Guidelines is not intended to question the expertise, integrity or dedication of primary investigators working their cases. Rather, it acknowledges years of research which concludes that even when utilizing precautions to avoid any inadvertent body signals or cues to witnesses, these gestures do occur when the identity of the actual suspect is known to the individual conducting the identification procedure. This provision of the Guidelines eliminates unintentional verbal

---

1. Of 40 cases analyzed, 36 of the subsequent exonerations involved convictions that were based on one or more erroneous eyewitness identifications. Wells, G. L., M. Small, S. D. Penrod, R. S. Malpass, S. M. Fulero, and C. A. E. Brimacombe. "Eyewitness Identification Procedures: Recommendations for Lineups and Photospreads." *Law and Human Behavior,* Vol. 22, No. 6. 1998.

and body cues which may adversely impact a witness' ability to make a reliable identification.

I recognize that this is a significant change from current practice that will not be possible or practical in every case. When it is not possible in a given case to conduct a lineup or photo array with an independent investigator, the primary investigator must exercise extreme caution to avoid any inadvertent signaling to a witness of a "correct" response which may provide a witness with a false sense of confidence if they have made an erroneous identification. Studies have established that the confidence level that witnesses demonstrate regarding their identifications is the primary determinant of whether jurors accept identifications as accurate and reliable.[2] Technological tools, such as computer programs that can run photo lineups and record witness identifications independent of the presence of an investigator, as well as departmental training of a broader range of agency personnel to conduct lineups and photo identifications may also assist agencies and departments with staff and budget constraints in implementing this recommendation.

The Guidelines also recommend that, when possible, "sequential lineups" should be utilized for both photo and live lineup identifications. "Sequential lineups" are conducted by displaying one photo or one person at a time to the witness. Scientific studies have also proven that witnesses have a tendency to compare one member of a lineup to another, making relative judgments about which individual looks most like the perpetrator. This relative judgment process explains why witnesses sometimes mistakenly pick someone out of a lineup when the actual perpetrator is not even present. Showing a witness one photo or one person at a time, rather than simultaneously, permits the witness to make an identification based on each person's appearance before viewing another photo or lineup member. Scientific data has illustrated that this method produces a lower rate of mistaken identifications.[3] If use of this method is not possible in a given case or department, the Guidelines also

---

2. Cutler, B.L., and S.D. Penrod. "Mistaken Identification: The Eyewitness, Psychology, and the Law," New York: Cambridge University Press, 1995; Wells, G.L. and Bradfield, A.L., "Distortions in Eyewitness Recollections: Can the Post-identification Feedback Effect be Moderated?", *Psychological Science*, 1999.

3. Wells, G.L., M. Small, S.D. Penrod, R.S. Malpass, S.M. Fulero, and C.A.E. Brimacombe. "Eyewitness Identification Procedures: Recommendations for Lineups and Photospreads." *Law and Human Behavior*, Vol. 22, No. 6., 1998.

provide recommendations for conducting simultaneous photo and live lineup identifications.

Although the Guidelines are fairly self-explanatory, their implementation will require a steep learning curve. To that end, training will be conducted. To accommodate appropriate training, the Guidelines will become effective within 180 days of the date of this letter. However, I would encourage you to implement the Guidelines sooner, if possible. I am requesting that each County Prosecutor designate key law enforcement personnel and police training coordinators to work with the Division of Criminal Justice to train your staff as well as the local law enforcement agencies within your jurisdiction.

While it is clear that current eyewitness identification procedures fully comport with federal and state constitutional requirements, the adoption of these Guidelines will enhance the accuracy and reliability of eyewitness identifications and will strengthen prosecutions in cases that rely heavily, or solely, on eyewitness evidence. The issuance of these Guidelines should in no way be used to imply that identifications made without these procedures are inadmissible or otherwise in error. Your cooperation is appreciated as all members of our law enforcement community strive to implement these procedures. Should you have any questions regarding the implementation of these Guidelines, please contact the Division of Criminal Justice, Prosecutors & Police Bureau, at (609) 984-2814.

Very truly yours,

John J. Farmer, Jr., Attorney General

Attachment

cc: Director Kathryn Flicker Chief of Staff Debra L. Stone Deputy Director Wayne S. Fisher, Ph.D. Deputy Director Anthony J. Zarrillo, Jr. Chief State Investigator John A. Cocklin SDAG Charles M. Grinnell, Acting Chief, Prosecutors & Police Bureau.

ATTORNEY GENERAL GUIDELINES FOR PREPARING AND CONDUCTING PHOTO AND LIVE LINEUP IDENTIFICATION PROCEDURES

PREAMBLE

While it is clear that current eyewitness identification procedures fully comport with federal and state constitutional requirements, that does not mean that these procedures cannot be improved upon. Both case law and recent studies have called into question the accuracy of some eyewitness identifications. The Attorney General, recognizing that his primary duty is to ensure that justice is done and the criminal justice system is fairly administered, is therefore promulgating these guidelines as "best practices" to ensure that identification procedures in this state minimize the chance of misidentification of a suspect.

I. COMPOSING THE PHOTO OR LIVE LINEUP

The following procedures will result in the composition of a photo or live lineup in which a suspect does not unduly stand out. An identification obtained through a lineup composed in this manner should minimize any risk of misidentification and have stronger evidentiary value than one obtained without these procedures.

A. In order to ensure that inadvertent verbal cues or body language do not impact on a witness, whenever practical, considering the time of day, day of the week, and other personnel conditions within the agency or department, the person conducting the photo or live lineup identification procedure should be someone other than the primary investigator assigned to the case. The Attorney General recognizes that in many departments, depending upon the size and other assignments of personnel, this may be impossible in a given case. In those cases where the primary investigating officer conducts the photo or live lineup identification procedure, he or she should be careful to avoid inadvertent signaling to the witness of the "correct" response.

B. The witness should be instructed prior to the photo or live lineup identification procedure that the perpetrator may not be among those in the photo array or live lineup and, therefore, they should not feel compelled to make an identification.

C. When possible, photo or live lineup identification procedures should be conducted sequentially, i.e., showing one photo or one person at a time to the witness, rather than simultaneously.

D. In composing a photo or live lineup, the person administering the identification procedure should ensure that the lineup is comprised in such a manner that the suspect does not unduly stand out. However, complete uniformity of features is not required.

E. Photo Lineup. In composing a photo lineup, the lineup administrator or investigator should:

1. Include only one suspect in each identification procedure.

2. Select fillers (nonsuspects) who generally fit the witness' description of the perpetrator. When there is a limited or inadequate description of the perpetrator provided by the witness, or when the description of the perpetrator differs significantly from the appearance of the suspect, fillers should resemble the suspect in significant features.

3. Select a photo that resembles the suspect's description or appearance at the time of the incident if multiple photos of the suspect are reasonably available to the investigator.

4. Include a *minimum* of five fillers (nonsuspects) per identification procedure.

5. Consider placing the suspect in different positions in each lineup when conducting more than one lineup for a case due to multiple witnesses.

6. Avoid reusing fillers in lineups shown to the same witness when showing a new suspect.

7. Ensure that no writings or information concerning previous arrest(s) will be visible to the witness.

8. View the array, once completed, to ensure that the suspect does not unduly stand out.

9. Preserve the presentation order of the photo lineup. In addition, the photos themselves should be preserved in their original condition.

F. Live Lineups. In composing a live lineup, the lineup administrator or investigator should:

1. Include only one suspect in each identification procedure.

   1. Select fillers (nonsuspects) who generally fit the witness' description of the perpetrator. When there is a limited or inadequate description of the perpetrator provided by the witness, or when the description of the perpetrator differs significantly from the appearance of the suspect, fillers should resemble the suspect in significant features.

2. Consider placing the suspect in different positions in each lineup when conducting more than one lineup for a case due to multiple witnesses.

3. Include a *minimum* of four fillers (nonsuspects) per identification procedure.

4. Avoid reusing fillers in lineups shown to the same witness when showing a new suspect.

II. CONDUCTING THE IDENTIFICATION PROCEDURE

The identification procedure should be conducted in a manner that promotes the accuracy, reliability, fairness and objectivity of the witness' identification. These steps are designed to ensure the accuracy of identification or nonidentification decisions.

A. Simultaneous Photo Lineup: When presenting a simultaneous photo lineup, the lineup administrator or investigator should:

1. Provide viewing instructions to the witness as outlined in subsection I B, above.

2. Confirm that the witness understands the nature of the lineup procedure.

3. Avoid saying anything to the witness that may influence the witness' selection.

4. If an identification is made, avoid reporting to the witness any information regarding the individual he or she has selected prior to obtaining the witness' statement of certainty.

5. Record any identification results and witness' statement of certainty as outlined in subsection II E, "Recording Identification Results."
    1. Document in writing the lineup procedure, including:
        1. Identification information and sources of all photos used.
        2. Names of all persons present at the photo lineup.
        3. Date and time of the identification procedure.

6. Instruct the witness not to discuss the identification procedure or its results with other witnesses involved in the case and discourage contact with the media.

B. Sequential Photo Lineup: When presenting a sequential photo lineup, the lineup administrator or investigator should:

1. Provide viewing instructions to the witness as outlined in subsection I B, above.
    1. Provide the following additional viewing instructions to the witness:
        1. Individual photographs will be viewed one at a time.
        2. The photos are in random order.
        3. Take as much time as needed in making a decision about each photo before moving to the next one.
        4. All photos will be shown, even if an identification is made prior to viewing all photos; or the procedure will be stopped at the point of an identification (consistent with jurisdictional/departmental procedures).

2. Confirm that the witness understands the nature of the sequential procedure.

3. Present each photo to the witness separately, in a previously determined order, removing those previously shown.

4. Avoid saying anything to the witness that may influence the witness' selection.

5. If an identification is made, avoid reporting to the witness any information regarding the individual he or she has selected prior to obtaining the witness' statement of certainty.

6. Record any identification results and witness' statement of certainty as outlined in subsection II E, "Recording Identification Results."
    1. Document in writing the lineup procedure, including:
        1. Identification information and sources of all photos used.
        2. Names of all persons present at the photo lineup.
        3. Date and time of the identification procedure.

7. Instruct the witness not to discuss the identification procedure or its results with other witnesses involved in the case and discourage contact with the media.

C. Simultaneous Live Lineup: When presenting a simultaneous live lineup, the lineup administrator or investigator should:

1. Provide viewing instructions to the witness as outlined in subsection I B, above.

2. Instruct all those present at the lineup not to suggest in any way the position or identity of the suspect in the lineup.

3. Ensure that any identification actions (e.g., speaking, moving, etc.) are performed by all members of the lineup.

4. Avoid saying anything to the witness that may influence the witness' selection.

5. If an identification is made, avoid reporting to the witness any information regarding the individual he or she has selected prior to obtaining the witness' statement of certainty.

6. Record any identification results and witness' statement of certainty as outlined in subsection II E, "Recording Identification Results."
    1. Document in writing the lineup procedure, including:
        1. Identification information of lineup participants.

2. Names of all persons present at the lineup.
3. Date and time of the identification procedure.

7. Document the lineup by photo or video. This documentation should be of a quality that represents the lineup clearly and fairly.

8. Instruct the witness not to discuss the identification procedure or its results with other witnesses involved in the case and discourage contact with the media.

D. Sequential Live Lineup: When presenting a sequential live lineup, the lineup administrator or investigator should:

1. Provide viewing instructions to the witness as outlined in subsection I B, above.
    1. Provide the following additional viewing instructions to the witness:
        1. Individuals will be viewed one at a time.
        2. The individuals will be presented in random order.
        3. Take as much time as needed in making a decision about each individual before moving to the next one.
        4. If the person who committed the crime is present, identify him or her.
        5. All individuals will be presented, even if an identification is made prior to viewing all the individuals; or the procedure will be stopped at the point of an identification (consistent with jurisdictional/ departmental procedures).

2. Begin with all lineup participants out of the view of the witness.

3. Instruct all those present at the lineup not to suggest in any way the position or identity of the suspect in the lineup.

4. Present each individual to the witness separately, in a previously determined order, removing those previously shown.

5. Ensure that any identification action (e.g., speaking, moving, etc.) are performed by all members of the lineup.

6. Avoid saying anything to the witness that may influence the witness' selection.

7. If an identification is made, avoid reporting to the witness any information regarding the individual he or she has selected prior to obtaining the witness' statement of certainty.

8. Record any identification results and witness' statement of certainty as outlined in subsection II E, "Recording Identification Results."
   1. Document in writing the lineup procedure, including:
      1. Identification information of lineup participants.
      2. Names of all persons present at the lineup.
      3. Date and time the identification procedure was conducted.

9. Document the lineup by photo or video. This documentation should be of a quality that represents the lineup clearly and fairly. Photo documentation can either depict the group or each individual.

10. Instruct the witness not to discuss the identification procedure or its results with other witnesses involved in the case and discourage contact with the media.

E. Recording Identification Results: When conducting an identification procedure, the lineup administrator or investigator shall preserve the outcome of the procedure by documenting any identification or non-identification results obtained from the witness. Preparing a complete and accurate record of the outcome of the identification procedure is crucial. This record can be a critical document in the investigation and any subsequent court proceedings. When conducting an identification procedure, the lineup administrator or investigator should:

1. Record both identification and nonidentification results in writing, including the witness' own words regarding how sure he or she is.

2. Ensure that the results are signed and dated by the witness.

3. Ensure that no materials indicating previous identification results are visible to the witness.

4. Ensure that the witness does not write on or mark any materials that will be used in other identification procedures.

   Dated: April 18, 2001, effective no later than the 180th day from this date.

APPENDIX D

Charlotte-Mecklenburg Police Department Eyewitness Identification Procedures

DIRECTIVES	Photographic Lineup Procedure	500-009	1 of 7
Effective Date	03/24/06		

 Charlotte-Mecklenburg Police Department
Interactive Directives Guide

I. PURPOSE

The purpose of this directive is to provide guidelines for preparing a non-suggestive photographic or body lineup for the purposes of eyewitness identification of a suspect involved in a police investigation.

II. POLICY

A lineup will be prepared in such a way that the suspect in the case does not unduly stand out from the other photographs or individuals in the lineup, in order to ensure reliable and accurate identifications. All personnel shall follow this policy when conducting photographic lineups.

III. DEFINITIONS

A. Sequential photographic lineup: An array of photographs, including the suspect and five (5) individuals who are similar in appearance, that are presented one at a time to a witness for identification purposes. The sequential lineup is the preferred method of presenting photographic lineups and will be used whenever a suitable array of photographs can be arranged in such a manner and can be presented by an independent administrator.

B. Simultaneous photographic lineup: A computer-generated array of photographs of individuals that includes the suspect and five (5) individuals who are similar in appearance that is presented on a single sheet of paper to a witness for identification purposes. A simultaneous lineup will be used whenever an independent administrator is not available or the circumstances are such that a sequential lineup cannot reasonably be utilized. An officer must obtain the approval of a supervisor before administering a simultaneous lineup.

C. Independent Administrator: An officer who does not know the identity of the suspect who has been placed in a sequential photographic lineup or a body lineup by the case investigator. An independent administrator will be used to administer a sequential photographic lineup whenever possible and will always be used to administer a body lineup.

D. Body lineup: A non-suggestive display of individuals that includes the suspect and five (5) individuals who are similar in appearance and who are presented one at a time to a witness for identification purposes; often referred to as a physical or live lineup.

E. Fillers: Individuals or photographs of individuals that resemble the suspect that are used to fill in a lineup. A minimum of five (5) fillers will be used with any simultaneous or sequential lineup. Individuals who are suspects in the same case may not be used as fillers.

F. Witness: A person, including a victim, who views a photographic or body lineup.

IV. PROCEDURE

A. Sequential Photographic Lineup.

A sequential lineup will be the preferred method of preparing and presenting a photographic lineup. Photographs may be generated using the CMPD mugshot system. A sequential lineup will also be used when the officer cannot prepare a lineup from the CMPD mug shot system and must rely upon photographs from outside sources. These sources may include yearbook photographs, Department of Motor Vehicles photographs or other sources providing photographs that are not compatible with conducting a simultaneous lineup. The officer will follow the guidelines listed below in creating the lineup in order to ensure that the suspect does not unduly stand out from the filler photographs used.

1. Only one suspect will be included in each lineup.

2. The suspect will not be placed in the first position of any lineup. The other members of the lineup will be placed randomly in the lineup. To the extent possible, the officer will place the suspect in different positions in each lineup when lineups will be shown to multiple witnesses in the same case.

3. The officer will select fillers who generally fit the witness' description of the perpetrator. When there is a limited or inadequate description of the perpetrator provided by the witness, or when the description of the perpetrator differs significantly from the appearance of the suspect, fillers should resemble the suspect in significant features.

4. The lineup should maintain a consistent similarity of appearance between the suspect and fillers with respect to any unique or unusual features such as scars or tattoos.

5. Complete uniformity of features is not required. The officer may avoid using fillers who so closely resemble the suspect that a person familiar with the suspect might find it difficult to distinguish the suspect from the fillers.

6. The officer will ensure that no writings or information concerning previous arrests or identifications will be visible to the witness on any lineup.

7. The officer will view the lineup once it is completed to ensure that the suspect does not unduly stand out and appears only once in the lineup.

8. Photographs will be shown to the witness one at a time by an independent administrator. If an independent administrator cannot be used, the case investigator will prepare a simultaneous lineup.

9. The officer will show the witness all of the photographs in the lineup, even if the witness makes an identification early in the procedure.

10. If the witness requests to see a specific photo after being shown the entire array, the officer will show the entire array to the witness again, in the same order in which it was initially presented.

11. If the nature of the photographs will not allow for a simultaneous presentation and an independent administrator is not used, the case investigator may present the sequential lineup and must exercise extreme caution to avoid inadvertent signaling to the witness of the "correct" response.

12. When showing a lineup with a different suspect, the officer will not use the same fillers used in previous lineups shown to the same witness.

B. Simultaneous Photographic Lineup.

A simultaneous lineup may only be conducted with a supervisor's approval. The officer should document the need to conduct a simultaneous lineup and the approving supervisor in a supplement. A simultaneous lineup will be constructed using photographs available from the CMPD's mug shot system. If a viable photo of the suspect is not available in the CMPD system, a lineup may be generated using other sources that provide similar photographs of every individual to be used in the array. A lineup consisting of photographs provided by other agencies or data sources will be utilized only if it satisfies this directive's requirement of fairness and reliability. In composing a photographic lineup, the officer will adhere to the following guidelines:

1. Only one suspect will be included in each lineup.

2. The suspect will not be placed in the first position of any lineup. The other members of the lineup will be placed randomly in the lineup. To the extent possible, the officer will place the suspect in different positions in each lineup when lineups will be shown to multiple witnesses in the same case.

3. The officer will select fillers who generally fit the witness' description of the perpetrator. When there is a limited or inadequate description of the perpetrator provided by the witness, or when the description of the perpetrator differs significantly from the appearance of the suspect, fillers should resemble the suspect in significant features.

4. The lineup should maintain a consistent similarity of appearance between the suspect and fillers with respect to any unique or unusual features such as scars or tattoos.

5. Complete uniformity of features is not required. The officer may avoid using fillers who so closely resemble the suspect that a person familiar with the suspect might find it difficult to distinguish the suspect from the fillers.

6. The officer will ensure that no writings or information concerning previous arrests or identifications will be visible to the witness on any lineup.

7. The officer will view the lineup once it is completed to ensure that the suspect does not unduly stand out and appears only once in the lineup.

8. When showing a lineup with a different suspect, the officer will not use the same fillers used in previous lineups shown to the same witness.

C. Conducting a Photographic Lineup.

A sequential or simultaneous lineup will be conducted in a manner that promotes reliability, fairness, and objectivity in the identification process.

1. The officer will give the witness verbal instructions regarding the lineup. In addition, the officer will give the witness a written copy of the Simultaneous Photographic Lineup Instruction Sheet and have the witness sign an acknowledgement of receipt. If multiple witnesses are involved, the officer will separate the witnesses and give each witness instructions regarding the lineup without the other witnesses present. Witnesses should not be allowed to confer with one another either before, during, or after the procedure.

2. The officer will instruct the witness prior to viewing the lineup that the suspect may or may not be included in the lineup. When conducting a sequential lineup, the officer will not inform the witness: 1) how many photographs will be shown in the lineup, or 2) prior to the complete lineup presentation, that the witness will be allowed to view the lineup a second time if they do not make identification.

3. The officer will instruct the witness that it is as important to eliminate innocent parties from consideration as it is to identify those involved in the crime.

4. The officer will instruct the witness that characteristics such as hairstyles, beards and mustaches can easily be changed and that complexions may look slightly different in photographs.

5. The officer will instruct the witness that, upon viewing the lineup, the witness will be asked if they recognize anyone and if so, the circumstances from which the witness recognizes the individual.

6. Prior to showing the lineup, the officer will ask the witness if they understand how the procedure will be conducted and if they have any questions.

7. The witness will then be given the opportunity to view the lineup. To the extent possible, the lineup will be placed before the witness in such a way that the officer is not holding or touching the lineup while the witness is viewing the lineup.

8. The witness may look at the lineup for as long as the witness wishes; however, the officer may not provide any feedback regarding the photographs.

9. If the witness indicates that they recognize someone in the lineup, the officer will ask the circumstances from which the witness recognizes the individual. The officer will document the witness' responses for the investigative case file. When conducting a sequential lineup, the officer will show the witness all of the photographs, even if the witness makes identification during the presentation.

10. If the witness identifies anyone in the lineup, the witness will be asked to sign and date the lineup or photograph, indicating the individual

they identified. The lineup will become a part of the investigative case file.

11. If the witness identifies a suspect, the officer will not provide the witness any feedback regarding the individual selected or comment on the outcome of the procedure in any way.

12. The officer will instruct the witness not to discuss the lineup or its results with other witnesses and will discourage the witness from discussing the case with the media.

13. In the event there are multiple witnesses, each witness will be shown a clean copy of the lineup.

14. The officer will document all lineup procedures, including the source of the photos used, the date and time the lineup was conducted, and the names of all persons present when the lineup was shown. Any lineup that an officer shows to a witness, regardless of whether or not the witness makes an identification of the suspect, will become a part of the investigative case file and, in the case of a sequential lineup, will include documentation as to the order in which the photos were shown to the witness.

D. Body Lineups

A body lineup will be used most often in situations where an individual who is a suspect in multiple cases is in custody or in a case where numerous witnesses may be able to identify the suspect. If the suspect is not in custody, the suspect may be asked to voluntarily participate in a lineup or may be required to participate through the use of a nontestimonial identification order. A body lineup will be conducted at the Mecklenburg County Jail Central facility and will be coordinated with the Mecklenburg County Sheriff's Office, in order to ensure that the suspect is not scheduled for a court appearance and will be available at the facility in a timely manner. A body lineup will be conducted under the guidance of a supervisor from the Criminal Investigations Bureau. An officer conducting a body lineup will adhere to the following guidelines.

1. All witnesses will be required to appear at the CMPD Headquarters Building at least one hour before the lineup, in order to ensure their presence and to provide them with instructions regarding the lineup.

2. The District Attorney's Office will be notified of the lineup, so that the appropriate Assistant District Attorney may attend.

3. The suspect's attorney (or the Public Defender's Office, when appropriate) will be notified on the day of the lineup at least three (3) hours prior to the lineup.

4. The officer will request a meeting with the suspect and his attorney prior to the lineup, in order to provide adequate time for lineup preparation.

5. The suspect and his attorney will be given the opportunity, under escort of detention personnel, to select nine (9) individuals from the inmate population to serve as fillers in the lineup. The officer will then select five (5) of those individuals as fillers.

6. The officer will ensure that each of the fillers is dressed similarly to the suspect and that the lineup participants represent a non-suggestive lineup.

7. The suspect will not be placed in the first position of any lineup. If only one witness is viewing the lineup, the suspect and his attorney will be allowed to place the participants in the order in which they wish them to appear in the lineup. If multiple witnesses are involved, the officer will, to the extent possible, place the suspect in different positions in each lineup. The other members of the lineup will be placed randomly in each lineup.

8. Each participant will be given a visible number corresponding to their placement in the lineup and numbers will be exchanged as the participants' positions in successive lineups change.

9. A photograph of each lineup will be taken prior to its presentation, documenting the order in which the participants are presented and their clothing and general appearance.

10. An independent administrator will give instructions to the witnesses and conduct the lineup. The case investigator will not have contact

with the independent administrator or the witnesses. The same procedures for separating witnesses, providing instructions, and administering the lineup, as set forth in Section IV.C.1 – 6 above, will be followed.

11. Prior to the viewing the lineup, the witness will be instructed that they will be looking at a series of individuals, one at a time, through a two-way mirror and that the individuals will not be able to see or hear the witness.

12. Upon entering the viewing area, the witness will be given the opportunity to view the participants, one at a time, from the front and from the side. If it is necessary for the participants to perform any physical actions (speak a phrase, walk, etc.), each participant must perform the same actions.

13. After viewing all of the participants, the witness will be asked if they recognize anyone in the lineup. If the witness recognizes anyone, the witness will be asked to state the circumstances from which the witness recognizes the individual. All of the participants will be brought into the viewing area, even if the witness makes identification during the presentation. The suspect's attorney will not be allowed to question any witness.

14. If the witness requests to see a specific individual after viewing the entire lineup, the officer will present the entire lineup to the witness again, in the same order in which it was initially presented.

15. If the witness identifies a suspect, the officer will not provide the witness any feedback regarding the individual selected or comment on the outcome of the procedure in any way.

16. After a witness has viewed the lineup, the officer will instruct the witness not to discuss the lineup or its results with other witnesses and will discourage the witness from discussing the case with the media.

17. The officer will record the results of the lineup on the body lineup form and will include the exact words used by each witness in viewing the lineup. The officer will also prepare a detailed supplement as to how the proceeding was conducted. The officer will maintain the body lineup form and the supplement in the investigative case file and forward copies to the District Attorney's Office.

V. REFERENCES

NIJ Guidelines "Eyewitness Evidence – A Guide For Law Enforcement" October 1999

North Carolina Actual Innocence Commission Recommendations for Eyewitness Identification

North Carolina Department of Justice: "Recommendations For Eyewitness Identification"

APPENDIX E

Denver Police Department Standard Operating Procedure and Training Bulletin for Videotaping Interrogations

TRAINING BULLETIN

BY JONATHYN W. PRIEST

DENVER POLICE DEPARTMENT

CRIMES AGAINST PERSONS BUREAU

VIDEO INTERVIEW FACILITY
VIDEO INTERVIEW TECHNIQUES

(The following pages are excerpts of the full training bulletin. Other components include technical instruction to use the rooms and equipment as well as protocols for interviewing other parties.)

The Denver Police Department has been videotaping homicide and serious crime scenes since 1979. Videotaping has been used to document line-ups, surveillance activities, witness hypnosis sessions, search warrant execution, and a myriad of other activities. Video recordings provide a clear and accurate record of police activities as well as interviews. The video recording of interviews has occurred in Denver since November of 1983 when members of the Denver Police Department and the Denver District Attorney's Office joined in the development and implementation of a Video Interview facility and procedure for video interviewing.

This early facility consisted of a single interview room with a camera room located behind a two-way mirror. Viewing the interview was made possible by way of a remote monitor located in a third room. Video recording interviews in Denver was born.

This system quickly became the premier procedure for documenting and preserving statements from victims, witnesses and suspects. Officer involved shooting investigations as well as homicide investigations occupied a great deal of time in this room. Through the years it became increasingly obvious that the need for an additional room was necessary.

In the third quarter of 1995, a plan was developed to expand the video interview facility as well as incorporate state of the art equipment for video capture. In January of 1997, the new facility was ready for use. The new facility system now consists of two separate interview rooms connected to a central recording equipment room. In addition, there are two viewing rooms with the capability of viewing interviews being conducted in the interview rooms from a single location. Additionally, a computer monitor screen was added to each interview room and connected to a remote computer terminal. This will allow viewers outside the room to send questions to the interviewer without disturbing the conversation.

While the primary use of these rooms is for the documentation of statements and confessions of persons involved in serious crimes, the rooms are also used for many other purposes. Young victims of sexual assault or child abuse are interviewed on videotape thereby avoiding needless repetition of painful testimony to other police personnel, prosecutors, parents, and social workers. Statements of hostile or uncooperative witnesses, who may recant at a later date, are preserved for subsequent use in court should their initial account change. Furthermore, the viewing and documentation of the recovery of evidence, execution of non-testimonial court orders, and clothing a witness is wearing can be facilitated.

Statement taking has long been a process of verbal interviewing followed by a set of questions and answers, then reducing the process to writing. Stenographers and tape recordings became more prevalent in the 70's, with low tech videotaping in the 80's. Today's technology allows for the much superior multi-purpose, digital capture available.

Tape recordings and stenographers provided a clear and accurate record of what was said, however, the video recording has many distinct advantages. These include, but are not limited to:

- Clothing being worn by the subject.

- Demeanor and actions are easily viewed.

- Injuries present, or the lack of the same, are clearly evident.

- Body language, eye movement and other non-verbal gestures are seen and can be evaluated.

- Mental and physical conditions at the time of the interview are better preserved.

- This format further provides a forum for the individuals to "show" what happened, use diagrams to augment statements as well as clarify testimony with demonstrations and exhibits.

The video is an aid to the investigation, during their preparation and presentation of a criminal case. These tapes can be viewed by:

1. Investigators, not present at the initial interview.

2. Prosecutors, who must make filing decisions and introduce the case in court.

3. Judges, who must make legal decisions.

4. Defense attorneys, who must go to trial or decide at what level to plead a client.

5. Psychiatrists, who may provide an opinion related to the mental state of a subject.

6. Parents, social workers, and psychologists who must work with and treat the victims, witnesses and suspects of crimes.

7. The jurors, who will decide guilt or innocence of the accused.

Video recordings do not fade with time and have a perfect, unimpeachable memory. It reduces the number of witnesses who must testify concerning an event and may be more accurate than the collective recollection of all the witnesses who were present. Interviewers do not need to take notes or become distracted during the interview as the content is being documented completely. Recall and interpretation of what occurred may be augmented by later viewing of the interview. What order events happened, who participated in the event, the physical and mental condition of persons involved, the demeanor and attitudes of these participants, the questions asked, the answers given, or any non-verbal communication through body language and other gestures are all recorded as they happen.

Claims of improper conduct by the police, such as brutality, intimidation, threats, promises, or the failure to advise of constitutional rights, can be judged first hand by the viewer. A jury can be shown a particular interview and allowed to make their decision and what weight to give it when considering all the evidence. The video is also available for the appeals process and Superior Court review.

The use of these statements helps to reduce the time used testifying, time in suppression hearings as well as reduction in the number of witnesses called to give evidence. Video documentation will also assist in reducing evidence lost through suppression. Guilty pleas have increased, the likelihood of conviction has risen and the mental impact on victims and witnesses has been reduced, all through the use of this video medium.

"...A picture is worth a thousand words..." understates the true value of video recording with respect to the criminal justice system. There are no surprises, the video speaks, *and* demonstrates, for itself.

The use of this medium will continue to increase in the future. The courts have accepted this as a viable means of documenting testimonial information. Video documentation has proven its evidentiary value, ability to sway juries, and improved investigative integrity.

USING THE VIDEO INTERVIEW ROOM

Some of the various uses for the video interview facility include:

1. Statements, admissions and confessions of any suspects.

2. Officer Involved Shooting and Use of Force investigations

3. Statements from victims and witnesses of serious crimes, particularly where visible injury or emotional trauma is present. (Sex Assault, Child Abuse, Assault, Homicide, etc...)

4. Statements of "special" witnesses (hostile, uncooperative, witnesses to "jail house confessions," confidential informants, coconspirators who will testify for the prosecution, witnesses who may be unavailable at the time of court.)

THE DECISION TO VIDEO RECORD A STATEMENT

Video recording is not required by the laws in the State of Colorado. It is, however, expected by the jury who sit in the court during trial.

1. Police personnel are encouraged to use the *Video Interview Facility* when possible in taking statements or obtaining confessions from suspects involved in a crime.

2. The manner in which an investigator conducts their investigation and interrogation is left as flexible as possible to maximize effectiveness.

While the investigators are encouraged to video record statements, the individual investigator must use their professional judgment in making a determination as to what is performed and when it is completed.

3. General approaches include:[1]

    a. A subject is brought into the *Video Interview Facility* "cold" and recording begins immediately. This style fits with a suspect indicating a desire to confess. This may also work well with any suspect interview.

    b. The subject is interviewed in advance and then taken to the *Video Interview Facility* where the statement is documented electronically.

    c. The subject is interviewed in advance and then taken to the *Video Interview Facility* to "re-tell" the story to other investigators or District Attorney.

4. **Officer Involved Shooting** investigations utilize the *Video Interview Facility* more than any other investigation. Virtually all participants and witnesses are interviewed on video. Each interview conducted in relation to this investigation is scheduled in an order that will follow the best chronological order of the event. Interviews begin with civilian witnesses, followed by officer witnesses, and then involved officers. For more information about *Officer Involved Shooting investigations*, see the **Police Shooting Protocol**.

THE INTERVIEW ON VIDEO

Preparing for taking a video statement is the same as the preparation for completing any interview. Some areas become important as a result of the visual aspect associated with a video interview. As with any interview, the investigator should be familiar with, but not limited to, the following:

1. Basic facts and evidence relevant to the case.

2. Crime Scene: should you go there? Visits to the scene can be very helpful with respect to understanding a statement.

---

[1]. Although it is understood that some statements may be made off camera it is important to maintain consistency when obtaining testimony from victims, witnesses, and suspects.

3. What legally admissible evidence is available, and known, concerning the crime and the suspect? Identifying evidence and understanding its importance may become an issue should a statement be suppressed.

4. Has the suspect made prior statements either verbal or written? If so, have these statements available. They should be reviewed prior to an interview and used during the current interview.

5. Has the suspect been given a "Miranda warning?" How many times? In writing? By whom? If documented, have this information for your interview.

6. Has the suspect requested an attorney? This is an important fact to know prior to beginning a custodial interview.

7. Is the suspect a juvenile? A parent or guardian may be required prior to continuing.

8. Would a diagram of the scene be of use? Have someone familiar with the scene construct one. The plasma screens on the wall are for this purpose.

9. What defenses may be available or are likely to be raised at the time of trial? Be prepared to address issues these at the time of the interview.

10. Would physical evidence[2] to the crime be of assistance? Is it available for use?

Through proper preparation, the quality of the final product improves. Remember, you may have only one opportunity to interview the suspect, therefore, it is crucial that you cover all possible scenarios, ask all relevant questions, and most of all, get answers to those questions.

CONDUCTING THE INTERVIEW

Once the equipment setup is completed and the interview is about to begin, make the camera operator aware that you are ready. The operator

---

[2]. If you present evidence in the interview, use it toward the end of the interview so that should the statement be suppressed, the evidence section can be preserved and avoid editing problems.

will start the equipment and then knock on the glass, indicating that you may start. Wait a moment and begin your interview. Follow the Video Interview Sheet.

1. State the current date and time.

2. Introduce yourself. Title and name; I'm Detective John Jones.

3. State where you are located; "In the Video Interview Room and Denver Police Headquarters."

4. Describe what the interview concerns. (What is being investigated?)

5. Introduce who is being interviewed. (Subject)

6. Introduce others present in the room. (Other investigators, DA, Defense Council)

7. If the person being interviewed is a suspect you *may*[3] want to give the Miranda Advisement at this time.

8. Follow with the four (4) written questions:

    - Have any promises or threats been made at anytime by myself or anyone else to get you to make this statement?

    - Are you under the influence of any narcotics, drugs, or alcohol?

    - Is this statement being made voluntarily?

    - Are you aware that this is being both audio and video recorded? (see *video sheet*)

9. Use your professional interview skills to take a complete and thorough statement. Take your time and cover all areas completely. Remember that you may get only one chance at this.

10. The video capture equipment will record indefinitely to the capacity of the system hard disk. The audiocassettes will run indefinitely with the operator changing them as they reach the end.

---

[3]. You must decide at this time if the subject is in custody, or perceives custody. Many times this is simply a conversation and may not require Miranda. Be careful.

11. When the investigator concludes the interview, the concluding statement is left to the discretion of the interviewer. Many simply close by stating "this will conclude this statement." You may, however, want to ask a concluding statement like "often times, you are waiting to be asked a question so you can give a particular answer. During the interview, we may not have done this. Is there anything you believe we need to known in relation to this case?" Once completed simply conclude the interview and state the current date and time.

12. If, prior to conclusion, you need to stop the interview, for any reason, indicate the reason, if possible, and state the date and time you are stopping and that you are "going off the record." When you return, indicate the time and date and ask the interviewee if there was any conversation off the record. If so, discuss the conversation. It is also important to note any significant change in surroundings, clothing or other difference from one statement to the next when talking to the same individual.[4]

13. ***You should not discuss a suspect's criminal history on video. If you have a special circumstance, do it at the end of the interview where a break can be made. The purpose for this is that the jury is not allowed to view the suspect's prior criminal history.***

14. It is important to remember that others will see this video and/or listen to the audio portion of the interview. Often times the audiocassette is utilized for transcribing the interview. Conversation should be *one at a time*. Talking over or at the same time makes it difficult to understand what was said and who said it. Important facts are missed when this occurs. Ask the question, and then wait for the answer. If the subject pauses, wait a moment…then continue.

15. While conducting a video interview, questions should be direct and simple. Avoid compound questions, which may require compound answers. When wanting a description of events, ask open-ended questions. When you want a direct answer, ask close-ended questions.

---

[4]. If the subject changes clothing during the break, has evidence of medical treatment, is wearing/not wearing something that was/was not present during the previous interview, etc. The interviewer should address the discrepancy and why it occurred.

16. Don't mumble. Keep your subject from talking low, mumbling or slurring their speech. If you are covering important areas, you may wish to restate the subjects' answer. Think about your question before asking. Don't interrupt the subjects' answer unless it is advantageous to your interview. Don't anticipate an answer and then state it for the subject. Remember, this is their statement and they must answer.

USING THE VIDEO INTERVIEW IN COURT

The working "copy" should be used in court unless the defense demands the use of the "original" video kept with the original case file.

Should the "original" be used, take all pertinent precautions before, during and after use. The video equipment operator is an endorsed witness and will be available to testify in court if necessary. In most cases the video will be introduced by stipulation.

Videotape/DVD machines and television sets are available on moveable carts from the District Attorney's Office in room 492 at the City and County Building. These machines are simple to operate and may be used by the investigator who is showing or viewing the video. For court purposes, the DA will normally provide a technology and support person specifically trained in the use of this equipment. The Tech person will operate this equipment at time of the court hearing.

It is important to understand that the Video Interview Room system was specifically designed to capture a digital "original." Because of the digital nature of this capture, an infinite number of "copies" can be produced in the exact quality. If this process is properly explained, the use of the protected "original" will not be needed in court as the working "copy" will suffice.

PLASMA SCREENS

Each interview room contains a plasma screen with a "Smart Board" overlay. This system allows for the introduction of photographs and drawings of the scene to be introduced into the interview. Images that can be posted include, but are not limited to:

- Crime scene photographs

- Crime scene drawings
- Wound diagrams
- Injury photographs
- Photo lineups
- Video streams
- Vehicle photographs.

These digital images may then be "drawn" onto and the images captured on computers located in the equipment room. This process will substitute for drawings and posted information. The captured data can be reproduced for later demonstrative purposes.

APPENDIX F

Las Vegas Metropolitan Police Department Cold Case Solvability Criteria

LEVEL 1:

- Named suspect
- Forensic evidence (DNA, latent prints [AFIS], firearms)
- Witness identification of suspect
- Physical evidence that connects suspect to the victim. (Photographs, writing, fibers, etc.).

LEVEL 2:

- Unknown suspect
- Forensic evidence (DNA, latent prints [AFIS], firearms)
- Witness identification of suspect
- Physical evidence that connects suspect to the victim.

LEVEL 3:

- Unknown suspect
- Forensic evidence (DNA, latent prints[(AFIS], firearms)
- Physical evidence
- Witnesses unable to identify.

LEVEL 4:

- Unknown suspect
- Physical evidence
- Witnesses unable to identify
- Unidentified victim.

LEVEL 5:

- Unknown suspect
- Little or no physical evidence
- No witnesses
- Unidentified victim.

APPENDIX G

Washington, D.C., Metropolitan Police Department Homicide Case Review Solvability Chart

SUSPECT

Arrested but released ☐
Named, no arrest ☐
Incarcerated/other charge ☐
Under Investigation/
other charge ☐
Deceased ☐
Seen but unidentified ☐
No suspects ☐

COMMENTS

_____
_____
_____
_____
_____
_____
_____

WITNESS

Witness Under
Investigation/Trial ☐
Witness Incarcerated ☐
Multiple eye-witnesses ☐
Other ☐

_____
_____
_____
_____

FIREARM EVIDENCE

Shell Casings Recovered ☐
Slugs Recovered ☐

_____
_____

Linked to Another Crime ☐ _____

No Firearm Evidence
Recovered ☐ _____

FINGERPRINT EVIDENCE

Unidentified Prints
Recovered ☐ _____

No Fingerprint
Evidence Recovered ☐ _____

DNA EVIDENCE

Potential Suspect
DNA Recovered ☐ _____

Potential Probative
Victim DNA ☐ _____

No DNA Evidence
Recovered ☐ _____

OTHER CRIMES

Potential Link to
Another Crime ☐ _____

MISC. SOLVABILITY FACTORS

_____ ☐ _____
_____ ☐ _____

www.ingramcontent.com/pod-product-compliance
Lightning Source LLC
Chambersburg PA
CBHW051651170526
45167CB00001B/424